———◆———

"Everyone in this business longs to be able to tell some-body off; to get outraged, walk out the door, slam it behind them, and swear never to do business with 'those assholes' again. But the only way you can do this is if your mouth, throat, and stomach can swallow and digest feathers, beaks, and gnarly, wrinkled claws. Because sooner or later you're going to need something from 'those assholes' again. Sooner or later you'll find yourself in a situation where they are the only ones who can help you get your film made. And then what you have to do is eat every single bite of that nasty, dead crow you flung so joyously in their faces."

◆

WELCOME TO THE WORLD OF—

Tom DiCillo's

Living in Oblivion

◆

Tom DiCillo received his M.A. in directing from New York University's Graduate Film School in 1979. He then worked as a cinematographer, shooting eight feature films, including Jim Jarmusch's *Stranger Than Paradise*. In 1992 he was invited to the Sundance Institute as a Directing Fellow based upon his screenplay for *Johnny Suede*. He went on to direct the film, which won the Grand Prize at the 1991 Locarno International Film Festival. He won the 1995 Waldo Salt Screenwriting Award at the Sundance Film Festival for *Living in Oblivion,* which was chosen that year to open the Film Society of Lincoln Center's "New Directors/New Films" series at the Museum of Modern Art. He is currently in pre-production on his next film, *Box of Moonlight.* Tom DiCillo lives with his wife, Jane, on Manhattan's Upper West Side.

Living
in
Oblivion

—◆—

Tom DiCillo

A PLUME BOOK

PLUME
Published by the Penguin Group
Penguin Books USA Inc., 375 Hudson Street,
New York, New York 10014, U.S.A.
Penguin Books Ltd, 27 Wrights Lane,
London W8 5TZ, England
Penguin Books Australia Ltd, Ringwood,
Victoria, Australia
Penguin Books Canada Ltd, 10 Alcorn Avenue,
Toronto, Ontario, Canada M4V 3B2
Penguin Books (N.Z.) Ltd, 182-190 Wairau Road,
Auckland 10, New Zealand

Penguin Books Ltd, Registered Offices:
Harmondsworth, Middlesex, England

First published by Plume, an imprint of Dutton Signet,
a division of Penguin Books USA Inc.

First Printing, August, 1995
10 9 8 7 6 5 4 3 2 1

 REGISTERED TRADEMARK—MARCA REGISTRADA

ISBN 0-452-27599-7

Printed in the United States of America
Set in New Century Schoolbook
Designed by Stanley S. Drate/Folio Graphics Co., Inc.

For Jane

Acknowledgments

There are many people without whose support and generosity this film would never have been made. In particular, I would like to thank everyone who pitched in on "Part One," the spastic twitch that started it all. Financial contributions from the following samaritans enabled us to shoot this first half hour in five days: Dermot Mulroney, Frank von Zerneck, Robert Sertner, David Gil, Sheela Harden, Jane Gil, Hilary Gilford, Michael Griffiths, Danielle von Zerneck, James Fearnely, Matt Grace, Frank Prinzi and Ramon de Oliviera.

Equally generous was a gifted crew who worked for nothing, especially Stephanie Carroll, who was Production Designer on "Part One," and Dana Congdon, who edited it.

I am eternally indebted to Hilary Gilford and Michael Griffiths, whose financial leap of faith enabled me to finish the film as a feature. The unceasing efforts of my friend and Producer, Marcus Viscidi, were matched only by his patience during my frequent bouts with hysteria. I am equally indebted to Camilla Toniolo, Editor; Therese Deprez, Production Designer; Ellen Lutter, Costume Designer; Frank Prinzi, Director of Photography; Meredith Zamsky, Co-producer; and Bill Bettencourt, Still Photographer, who gamely stood in for every one of the actors when he wasn't taking the spectacular photographs that appear in this book.

My personal thanks and admiration go to all the actors whose talent, trust, and daring made working with them a delight. Catherine Keener's humor and unflinching commitment to honesty were essential inspirations for the film.

Stephen Pevner was crucial to the creation of this book, not only for his clarity in helping me organize my notes but for his passionate belief in both the diary and the film. His thoughtful gifts of a bullet-proof vest and the cookbook, "Tasty Crow Recipes I've Known and Loved," will be much appreciated after this book is published.

It is however to Jane Gil that I owe my greatest debt. Her love, faith, and courage have inspired me for a long, long time.

Introduction

I never set out to make a movie about filmmaking; it just happened. I'm not fixated on my profession, nor do I feel people in it are automatically interesting as subjects of scrutiny and self-adoration. This screenplay, the resulting film, and this diary, are the results of an accidental and unexpected step into the mirror.

Ironically, the screenplay emerged at a time when I was the most disillusioned with every aspect of the filmmaking process; from raising the money to the technical nightmares of shooting. Making the film restored my faith. It also made me look back on my eighteen years of low-budget filmmaking with a greater respect and admiration for all the crazy people I've worked with who had no money, no equipment, no food, nothing but the manic desire to achieve the impossible: to capture something beautiful on film.

Author's Note

Caution: This diary is an extremely unstable mixture of Truth and Fiction. Although every event actually occurred, and every word of dialogue was actually spoken, names and places have been changed to protect the innocent. Anyone attempting to identify other people will be slapped. Anyone attempting to recognize themselves will be spanked. Anyone taking offense will be avoided.

Eating Crow

Notes from a Filmmaker's Diary

◆

Dec. 22, 1994

I was on the set of *Living in Oblivion* today; we were about to film a very important scene involving delicate, emotional commitment from the actress, Catherine Keener, and extreme attention to the camera move. Catherine was ready, the camera move rehearsed to perfection, and we were just about to shoot when I realized I had to take a leak.

"I'll be right back," I yelled to the Assistant Director, and ran down the hall to the bathroom. To my irritated surprise, the door was locked. After asking a stranger standing in the hall I learned there was another bathroom on a lower floor. The doorway to this floor was at the end of a long, twisting corridor and as I rushed down it, I somehow took a wrong turn and got lost. It was over an hour before I found the bathroom, took a leak and got back to the set.

As I ran in, I noticed the crew was just standing around in boredom. Catherine was gone and the camera had been broken down and put away.

"OK!" I said. "Let's shoot."

The AD just looked at me and said, "We already did the shot, Tom."

"You did the shot?!"

"Yes," the AD stated. "We shot it while you were gone."

"How did it go?" I asked, approaching hysteria.

"Oh, so-so," came the dispassionate reply.

I suddenly woke up in bed, in my apartment. After a moment I looked at the clock. It was 4:00 A.M. I can't believe I'm still having Anxiety Dreams eight months after making the film that I thought would exorcise them from me forever.

Finally fell back to sleep around 6:30 and got woken at 10:00 by a phone call. It was from Kelly Gordon, a woman who runs the film series at the Smithsonian's Hirshhorn Museum in DC. She'd heard about the film from someone who'd been at my Cast and Crew screening in November. She offered me $1,200 to show *Living in Oblivion* there in March 1995. I feigned indifference and accepted immediately. That $1,200 will be my first income since September 1994. At the moment my bank balance is hovering at $5,900. If we indeed sell the film at Sundance in January and Berlin in February, I will most likely be broke before I see a cent.

◆

Dec. 24, 1994

Went to a Christmas party and ran into Ira Deutchman, the head of Fine Line, and Bob Aaronson, Fine Line's VP of Acquisitions. Bob pulled me aside and said he'd heard great things about the movie.

"When can I see it?" he asked.

"Not till Sundance, Bob," I said. "I'm not showing it to any distributors before then."

Just then he introduced me to Amy, a woman who used to be his assistant but who now works for Miramax. Miramax has also called, wanting to see the film, so I explained my strategy to both of them.

"It's very important to me that *Living in Oblivion* gets seen," I said. "*Johnny Suede* (my first film) opened in NY in the dead of August and was pulled from the theater after less than three weeks. If that happens with *Living in Oblivion*, I'll probably never get a chance to make another movie. So, I figured the best way to find a distributor for this film is to show it to them all at the same time, the way it was meant to be seen—with a real audience. Then, based on our sense of who best understands the film, and who most believes in it, we'll make our decision."

Although Bob and Amy agreed with this, they both pointed out the merits of securing a distributor before we go to Sundance.

"That way you could have the power of a distributor behind

you at the Festival," Amy stated. "Setting up press, doing publicity; that's very important, you know."

"I had the power of a distributor behind me when I was at Sundance with *Johnny Suede*," I said. "The only press materials they provided for the film were badly xeroxed copies of a Press Book I had written for the Locarno Film Festival, a year earlier. Which I wouldn't have minded except every word was in French."

I laughed briefly, remembering this funny episode. However, I stopped quickly, seeing Amy's cold stare. Now that I think about it, I probably shouldn't have told Bob and Amy the Press Book story. In fact, I'm a little angry at myself. I'm writing a book about this business called *Eating Crow*. Christ, I just finished Chapter 19, "Insulting Distributors: First Step to Career Suicide," and there is no excuse for my lapse of reason.

The basic premise of *Eating Crow* is this: Everyone in this business longs to be able to tell somebody off; to get outraged, walk out the door, slam it behind them, and swear never to do business with "those assholes" again. But the only way you can do this is if your mouth, throat, and stomach can swallow and digest feathers, beaks, and gnarly, wrinkled claws. Because sooner or later you're going to need something from "those assholes" again. Sooner or later you'll find yourself in a situation where they are the only ones who can help you get your film made. And then what you have to do is eat every single bit of that nasty, dead crow you flung so joyously in their faces.

———◆———

Jan. 4, 1995

The holidays are over. Winter has finally hit NYC; it's nineteen degrees out. Just paid the rent and end-of-month bills. Bank balance now $5,000. I have finished my next script, *The Real Blonde* and I don't leave for Sundance until the 23rd. I have 2½ weeks of empty time and I'm not quite sure what to do with myself.

I keep saying that one of these days I will go sit in the closet for a couple hours and prepare myself emotionally for Sundance. As much as I respect the Festival's commitment to Independent Film, it is obvious to everyone that success at Sundance is the golden apple that opens the backdoor to Hollywood. Consequently, the vying for attention and the vying to be with those getting that attention has the manic, ruthless fervor of a High School Homecoming Queen election.

Nonetheless, it is the premier festival in the US for independent film. It attracts all the independent US distributors, as well as major studios and foreign distributors. The unspoken word is that the Audience Award is the prize to get. Since *Sex, Lies, and Videotape*, no film to win the Grand Jury Prize has gone on to a successful commercial release. *In the Soup*, winner when *Johnny Suede* was there, was bought by a small distribution company that almost immediately went bankrupt. *Reservoir Dogs*, at the same festival, was completely ignored by the Jury as was *Johnny Suede*. The chill of dismissal, compounded by the frigid temperatures, can make the place pretty bleak. After my last experience there, I swore I was never going back. (See *Eating Crow*, Chapter 7, "Bad-mouthing Festivals: Heresy, Idiocy, or Both?")

◆

Jan. 6, 1995

Met with Mark Urman today, a publicist at Dennis Davidson Associates in New York. We're considering hiring him to handle publicity at Sundance. Since we have so much riding on this one festival, the expense seems worth the risk.

The only major US festivals between Toronto (August) and Sundance (January) are the Hamptons and the New York Film Festivals. I had wanted to go to Toronto, but we missed the deadline by a week. After talking it over with my producers, we decided to wait the six months and take our chances on getting into Sundance.

However, in early September, word about the film got to both Daryl McDonald at the Hampton Festival and Richard Peña at New York. Their requests to see the film aroused my anxieties that I perhaps should submit to both festivals and not wait for Sundance. McDonald officially invited the film and expected an answer from me quickly. His enthusiasm for the film was so genuine it was extremely difficult to say no.

The New York Film Festival was another story entirely. The film was still in its work print stage at the time Peña wanted to see it (splices, unmixed, no credits). I was nervous about showing Peña the film at this stage. I had shown *Johnny Suede* in a similar stage to the Cannes selection committee three years earlier. Two months after they rejected it, the film won Best Picture at Locarno. A guy who had been on the Cannes committee came rushing up to me and exclaimed, "My God! The changes you made in the film are incredible!"

The only change I had made in the film was that it had been mixed and printed. Not a frame of picture, dialogue, or music had been cut, added, or moved.

Nonetheless, due to the prestige the New York Film Festival carries, we decided to show Peña the film. We rented a screening room and invited a few people, most of whom did not show up. As a result, the room was almost empty. Those who did come said afterwards they felt afraid to laugh because they thought other people would "look at them funny." It was a completely dead screening.

Surprisingly, Peña's reaction to the film was favorable enough for him to make a formal request to show it to the rest of the committee. Again, based upon what seemed to be his enthusiasm, I submitted the film unfinished, on videotape. It was rejected.

Flashback—Sept. 4, 1993

Financing for my film, Box of Moonlight *just fell apart for the fifth time. I'm convinced now it's never going to happen. It was supposed to have been my second feature. I've spent three years trying to make it.*

I'm now writing a short film. The idea struck me over the weekend when Jane and I went to her cousin Hilary's wedding. At the reception I had a couple martinis and noticed this guy who kept looking at me. I couldn't tell if I knew him or if the alcohol was making everyone my friend. It ends up I did know him. Ryan was in one of my acting classes eight years ago. He was wildly congratulatory to me about having made Johnny Suede. *He kept saying how exciting it must have been, working with actors, the lights, the cameras, all the glamour stuff. Finally, I interrupted him.*

"Listen Ryan, I don't want to sound funny, but most of the time making a movie is the most tedious, boring bunch of shit you can imagine. Especially for the actor; it can be an emotional nightmare. You might be all ready for a scene, your preparation is working, you're ready to fly and out of nowhere a light goes off, a car radio comes on, someone sneezes. And that moment you had—that fragile, rare moment of truth—is gone forever. It's a nightmare."

"Are you serious?" Ryan asked, his mouth hanging open.

"Absolutely serious," I replied, forking another martini from a passing waiter's tray. It was somewhere after that martini that the idea hit me.

I've sketched out a short film based upon what I told Ryan; a typical day on the set, an actress trying to do one scene, her downward spiral of concentration as everything goes wrong. A microphone dips into frame, a light explodes, the AC loses focus, some kind of beeping sound no one can locate.

Flashback—Oct. 6, 1993

I've finished the short script. It's called "Scene 6, Take 1," and would probably make a 25-minute film. I showed it to Catherine Keener, who just spent five days with us. We've become good friends since I cast her in Johnny Suede *and I know she'd be incredible as The Actress. She responded to the script with spasms of laughter. We must have said, "We should make this!" at least twenty times during her visit. We've talked about shooting it in 16mm, everyone working for free, some-*

*how raising the money; the excitement is high—the specifics
are extremely vague. Today when Catherine left, we all stood
in the doorway, Jane, Catherine, and I, and our last words to
each other were, "We're going to make this."*

*Yet even as I stood there saying, in a voice of firm, resolute
conviction, "Listen, we're not just talking here; we really are
going to make this movie," part of me was thinking, "What
are you talking about? You don't have any money; you don't
even have enough to shoot this on super 8. Look how many
times you said you were going to make* Box of Moonlight *and
where the hell is that?"*

◆

Jan. 7, 1995

Thought of a way to generate a little income. Opened my
plastic Bob's Big Boy coin bank and packed my change into
paper denomination rolls. I had 120 quarters, 200 dimes, and
200 nickels; which I took to the bank and converted into $60
cash. I saw no sense in depositing this into my checking account which is now at a balance of $4,600.

◆

Jan. 8, 1995

Had a call from Joe Spaniel, an agent at Artistic Artists.
AA refused to sign me as an actor seven years ago but
offered to work with me "freelance" on an unofficial basis. I
never had a single audition through them. Now Joe wanted to
get together.

"Why?" I said.

"Just to catch up," Joe said.

"On what?" I asked.

Here Joe hesitated. "I'll be honest with you, Tom."

"Good," I said.

"We like you. We want to help you."

"Help me what?" I asked.

"Let's talk about that over lunch. I'd like you to meet Larry Suckling, the head of the agency. How's Friday look?"

"Well, Friday's OK, Joe, but I'm just a little confused what we'll be talking about. You know, I already have an agent."

"We know that, Tom. That's not what this is about at all."

"Oh, I see. What is it about?"

Here Joe hesitated again. "We would just like to keep in touch," he said finally. "Nothing more than that. We like you, we like your movie; that's all. I just wanted to let you know if you ever need anything, just call me. Don't be a stranger. I'm here for you, man. Just because we don't represent you doesn't mean anything. Bottom line, we're friends. Right?"

"Yeah, no. You're right," I said.

"Good, because when you go out to Sundance, Tom, it's going to be crazy, it's going to be chaotic. You're going to need someone to talk to. Because people are going to be all over you. They'll be coming out of the woodwork, like cockroaches, like termites; they'll be crawling all over you."

"Like you are right now?" I asked.

Here Joe hesitated for a very long time. Actually, Joe didn't hesitate, because I didn't say, "Like you are right now?" Instead I referred to *Eating Crow*, Chapter 3, "Agents As People," and said, "Thanks a lot, Joe, I really appreciate this."

And Joe said, "Let me know about Friday," and he hung up.

◆

Jan. 9, 1995

Had some bad news; Steve Buscemi called and said it didn't look good for him coming to Sundance. He just got a big part in the new Coen Brothers movie and they start shooting January 20th in Minneapolis.

Steve's trust and willingness as an actor were completely rejuvenating for me. Whenever I suggested something, he always said, "OK." If he didn't like a suggestion he came up with something to make it better. He never shut down on me; he was constantly, totally engaged. I think it is his best work in a movie. I am very disappointed he won't be there to enjoy the American premiere of the film.

Flashback—Nov. 12, 1993

I'm a little bit in shock; we're supposed to start shooting "Scene 6, Take 1" in a week. After cutting every financial corner in existence, I've come up with a budget of $35,000. It'll be a five-day shoot, with everyone working for free. The LA actors are paying their own airfare and putting themselves up. Plus, most of the actors are contributing to the budget. It's been an interesting way of casting; anyone who puts up money gets a part.

Here's how it happened: Catherine returned to LA in October 1993, and showed the script to her husband, Dermot Mulroney. Dermot immediately committed the first real money to the film, wanting to play Nick, the Director. I told him I'd imagined Nick as someone older, and suggested Wolf, the Cameraman for him. Without a trace of resentment Dermot said, "OK, what about Steve Buscemi for Nick?"

They'd just done a TV movie together and had become good friends. I've known Steve since the late 70s. I called him and to my amazement he immediately said "yes," he would act in the film, for nothing. He said it without reading the script. He did confess to me in rehearsal today that when he finally read the script three days later, he was somewhat relieved that it wasn't a total piece of shit.

Dermot's financial commitment triggered the rest of the money. My wife Jane raised $15,000 in four days. Her father put in $2,000, her cousin Hilary put in $5,000 for which she got the part of Script Girl. I gave her husband Michael the part of Speedo, the goateed Soundman. Jane's trainer Matt Grace put in $1,000 and I gave him the part of Les, the Boom Operator. He wants to play him as a white gangsta rapper. I told him he could, if he came up with another thousand. Out of gratitude to Ryan, my acting friend at Hilary's wedding, I gave him and his wife Francesca parts.

Several of Catherine and Dermot's friends have joined in. Danielle von Zerneck put up $2,000 and got the part of Wanda, the Assistant Director. She's also inspired her father, Frank von Zerneck and his partner, Bob Sertner, to put up $15,000 and to serve as Executive Producers.

Marcus Viscidi, who has been working so hard with me for three years on Box of Moonlight *will produce and Meredith Zamsky will line produce for nothing. Frank Prinzi has offered to shoot it for free and has donated $1,000 to the budget. My only disappointment is that we have to shoot 16mm. With this budget, shooting 35mm is completely out of the question.*

◆

Jan. 11, 1995

Had a call from Wendy Keys at The New Directors Series. She wants me to submit *Living in Oblivion* for their consideration. I'm nervous about the prospect of them "considering" the film and then passing on it the way the New York Film Festival did.

When I explained this to Wendy, she said unfortunately there were six other members of the selection committee who had to see the film. Several people have advised me to submit the film, based on the kind of exposure New Directors gets. Nonetheless, I'm not officially submitting the film until after Sundance.

The rejection by the New York Film Festival was tough. Even though they had also rejected *Johnny Suede* three years earlier, my faith in *Living in Oblivion* raised my hopes a little higher than I realized. An article in *The NY Times* covering the Festival helped put things in perspective. The article finds Harvey Weinstein, Demi Moore, Bruce Willis, and Quentin Tarantino sitting in a restaurant after a Festival screening of *Pulp Fiction*. The entire and only point of the article was the fact that they all (including Demi) were smoking cigars. I rushed immediately to the corner smokeshop for a box of cigars, but I had to wait in line for forty minutes because all the filmmakers in my neighborhood had gotten there before me.

———◆———

Jan. 12, 1995

Marcus came over today and we compiled our wish list of US distributors, in no particular order: Fine Line, Sony Classics, October, Miramax, Fox/Searchlight, and Goldwyn. All have strong points. Fine Line's done a great job finding the audience for *Hoop Dreams*, a three-hour documentary. Miramax is riding high right now off of *Pulp Fiction*. Some consider them the best independent distributor in the US. However, an article in the *NY Press* suggested Miramax has a tendency to drop films if they don't take off immediately at the box office. Sony, Fox, and Goldwyn are all solid distributors, as well as October, which has made a hit out of *The Last Seduction*.

Just after Marcus left, I had a call from Bob Aaronson at Fine Line. He told me all screenings of *Living in Oblivion* at Sundance are sold out, but he had managed to get tickets for the first screening there on the 19th. He also disturbed me by saying he had some things to tell me about some new developments at Fine Line.

———◆———

Jan. 13, 1995

Met this morning with Carol Myer from The Sales Co., an international sales agent. She wants to handle selling the film for Europe and has offered to do so "unofficially" until after Sundance, in the event a distributor there makes us a better offer for the world. She said we were up against two myths: 1. Films about filmmaking don't make any money. 2. Cinematographers turned directors don't make good films. I wasn't particularly thrilled about either of those comments; probably because I've heard them both before. However, I was very impressed with Carol's clarity and her passion for the film.

As she left, Carol said she was on her way to a meeting with Ira Deutchman, the head of Fine Line.

"To console him," she said.

"Console him for what?" I asked.

"He's just been fired. Ruth Vitale is taking his place."

I realized then what Bob Aaronson had wanted to tell me about Fine Line yesterday. Ira has run Fine Line for almost five years. Who knows what shape the company is in or how long Ruth Vitale will remain? The danger is that we sell the film to them and five months from now someone else takes over who has no personal or emotional interest in the film. This is very unsettling. They had been high on our list.

After the meeting with Carol, I went to the copy shop with my mock-up for the *Living in Oblivion* poster. I've designed a color layout to be laser-printed on 11 × 17 paper. This way we can make posters for the price of a color xerox.

Came home and had a phone call from someone named Trey Huckleberry at Universal Pictures.

"Just touching base with filmmakers going to Sundance," Trey said.

"Good, what's up?" I said in a voice I assumed would suggest I was open to base-touching.

"OK, that's it really," Trey said and hung up.

Mark Urman, our publicist, called to say he's set up a Press Screening on Wednesday, January 18th, in NYC. This screening is mainly for the New York press, including Janet Maslin from *The New York Times* who is covering Sundance this year. It will be the first time *Living in Oblivion* has been shown to critics and journalists.

I'm a little nervous about it. Every independent filmmaker and distributor in this country knows a bad review in *The New York Times* is literally the kiss of death. No one will go see the film. Most poorly reviewed independent films leave New York City theaters in a week.

It makes you wonder sometimes if critics think independent filmmakers live in a vacuum; that they can just make another movie whenever they feel like it. Are critics unaware that a bad review hurts *Hoop Dreams* in ways that it could never hurt *Dumb and Dumber*? For an independent film, every moviegoer turned away by a dismissive review is disastrous. The theater owners lose money, the distributors lose money, and the filmmaker loses any edge he or she may have had trying to convince someone to finance another film. Every moviegoer turned away by a bad review hurts the independent filmmaker in the most basic, primal way—survival, both economic and artistic.

"Critics are like soldiers who fire on their own troops." Jean Luc Godard, *Cahiers du Cinema*.

"I love critics more than life itself." Tom DiCillo, *Eating Crow*, Chapter 21.

Flashback—Nov. 28, 1993

We finished shooting "Scene 6, Take 1" on Friday. I am exhausted, exhilarated, and a little depressed.

Exhilarated, because the film turned out better than any of us could have expected. Depressed, because most likely no one is ever going to see this 16mm short film. The exhaustion needs no explanation.

We shot for five days in the dusty shadows of The Raw Space, a converted armory on 11th Ave. Everyone settled in to what we all assumed was just another freebie low-budget film. But about two days into filming, the atmosphere on the set suddenly changed.

Seeing the little 16mm camera, the minuscule crew, and a room full of actors who were my friends, my anxiety about the film's importance—about getting it "right"—disappeared. The whole thing suddenly became no more significant than a play put on in a garage by a bunch of neighborhood kids. There was no one telling us what to do, and there was literally nothing to lose except our time. Surprisingly, this atmosphere created the most efficient and exciting set I've ever been on.

It affected the actors, which in turn affected the crew. Most of the crew hadn't read the script (a fairly normal occurrence), but as soon as they began to see we were really telling their story, grips, electrics, and boom operators all began enthusiastically coaching the actors on how to do their jobs. They seemed to take real pleasure in showing their counterparts the "correct" way to hold the microphone, adjust a light, or push the dolly.

This interplay between illusion and reality became very clear one day when we were shooting a wide shot of the actor "crew" filming. I stepped off the set for a moment and when I returned I was startled by the sight of two movie cameras, facing each other, only inches separating their lenses. One was the real camera we were filming with, the other was the prop camera the actor filmmakers were using. Each camera had its matching film crew, all of whom were staring over at their opposites in silent concentration, creating a gigantic, living mirror image.

As originally written, the film was to end with Steve Buscemi tearing the set apart as he hunts for a mysterious beeping sound. This sequence was scripted as rather short, with only one shot of the astonished crew before he breaks down in a helpless scream. When it came time to film this shot, I asked Steve to stand off-camera and throw a few things around so the actors could have something to react to. I also told him he could yell at them if he wanted.

As we started filming, Steve watched Frank Prinzi focus on different members of the "crew" and he began lambasting them with specific, spontaneous insults related to how they each had contributed to his nightmarish day on the set.

The actors were as stunned as I was and the resulting "reaction" shots were priceless. As soon as we were done with the crew, I had Frank turn the camera around and I asked Steve to do it once more, this time on film. Not only did he match his previous intensity but he became even more demented in his

*insults. The whole scene was unrehearsed, completely impro-
vised by Steve and done in one take. At the end of it we all
applauded.*

*One element of the film had been giving me nightmares all
week: How to keep track of the fluctuating levels of "quality"
in Catherine Keener's performance. She was also concerned
about this. In Take One her "performance" had to be better
than her "performance" in Take Three. In Take Five her "performance" had to be better than Take Three, but worse than
Take Two. To help us both, I made a chart listing all the Takes
and, on a scale of 1–10, I gave them each a number, approxi-
mating their levels of quality.*

*However, right before we started shooting the takes, I lost
my little chart. Consequently, the subtle variations in Catherine's deteriorating performance were created mainly by her
improvisations and a few spontaneous suggestions of my own.
The only continuity we had was provided by the fact that we
shot these color "takes" all at the same time, one right after
the other. This was mainly due to time pressure and the
amount of color film we had.*

*It was funny to see the anxiety in our real crew when the
script called for them to intentionally screw up a shot. One
shot called for the real dolly-grip (an experienced professional)
to execute a wretched, shaky dolly move. Take after take, the
grip would only halfheartedly botch the move until finally I
grabbed the dolly and showed him exactly what I wanted.*

"That bad?" he asked incredulously.

"The worse the better," I replied.

*I encountered the same hesitation from everyone—the AC's
reluctance to purposefully lose focus, the boomman's confusion when he was told to drop the mike into frame during a
shot. Everyone was so geared toward maintaining the sanctity
of the Frame, violating it was almost traumatic for them. Personally, I got a real kick out of doing it; it was like throwing a
rock through a school window.*

There's a crazy duality that exists on the set of every film. That duality being the simultaneous existence of what is going on in front of the camera, and what is going on behind it. It fascinates me that the behind-the-camera stuff—the massive concentration of chaos, noise, energy, and conflict—is generally not considered "real." What is "real" is the little scene all this energy is focused on. Ironically, most of the time this off-camera chaos is a million times more interesting and full of life than the scene being filmed.

Significantly, an inspiration for the film came from seeing Hearts of Darkness, *the documentary about the making of* Apocalypse Now. *Throughout that film, Coppola is seen darting wildly through his chaotic sets. He is sweating, dirty, and seems to be directing a sloppy, unorganized production that is only seconds away from self-destruction. Then the film cuts to the scene they were filming as it appeared in* Apocalypse Now *and I was overwhelmed by the lush, lyric beauty they had created from this chaos.*

To illustrate this contrast, I shot "Scene 6" in two different film stocks. The frenzied, cluttered world of the crew working was shot in grainy B/W, and the scene they were filming was shot in fine-grain, deeply saturated color. Using color for the scene would emphasize what I believe is every filmmaker's perception of their film; it is precious, magical; it exists in a realm all to itself.

On the last day of shooting, Catherine said to me jokingly, "Hey Tom, you ought to make this into a feature."

"Yeah, right," I said.

I start editing Monday. When it's done I guess I'll try to get it into a few short film festivals.

---◆---

Jan. 14, 1995

Heidi and Ingmar, a married couple from PAP Entertainment, a tiny distribution company based in Chicago, have been bugging me for weeks to have an "urgent" meeting with them. The urgency has to do with some important advice they want to give me regarding "marketing strategy at Sundance." When I suggested they just tell me the strategy over the phone, Heidi insisted it was so valuable it could only be given in person. Since they are leaving town tomorrow, today I finally gave in and agreed to meet them.

At the meeting, the strategy advice came down to Ingmar saying, "Sundance has changed drastically since you were there four years ago. The team you have working for you now seems unaware of this. Your postcard, poster, and press material are all weak and, frankly, the only way to save the film now is to let PAP distribute it. Our strategy would be to show it to distributors now and secure a deal before you go to Sundance."

This advice was presented along with a brochure about PAP Entertainment which revealed they had never distributed a feature film. Ingmar and Heidi further said they wanted to "rep" me and produce my next project. I thanked them for their interest but told them since I already had one lawyer, three agents, and three producers, there was no way to include them in my future plans. In spite of this, Ingmar wanted to know if he could "assist" us at Sundance in an "unofficial capacity." Since their enthusiasm for the film seemed genuine, I said, "Fine, as long as you know it's clear you are not connected to the film."

I came home and was immediately wracked with self-doubt about every aspect of our strategy in Sundance. I wanted to make new postcards, a new poster, and contemplated showing the film to distributors prior to going. I called Marcus who quickly brought me back to my senses.

Flashback—Feb. 17, 1994

Got the official word today; "Scene 6, Take 1" has been rejected by Cannes. Both the Short Film Competition and Un Certain Regard, one of the Festival sidebars have passed. I'm disappointed but not surprised. It only makes it more crucial that I finish the screenplay for the film as a feature.

I started the feature screenplay a month ago. The basic structure is a film in three parts, incorporating the short intact as Part 1. I've managed to finish Part 2, which is also a dream. It involves another slew of specific problems on the set, one of which I'm very excited about—tension between the Star Actor and the Director, which results in a fistfight right on the set.

Jane has given me a brilliant idea for Part 3. I was expressing my agony to her again yesterday about where the hell the story could go next and she said, "If Part 1 is a Dream, and Part 2 is a Dream, why don't you have Part 3 be about the crew shooting a dream sequence?"

I immediately thought of a smoke machine and a dwarf. The smoke machine will blow up and the dwarf will ridicule the Director in front of the entire crew for casting a dwarf in a dream sequence. I want the Director to give up completely at some point in Part 3, and this public humiliation could be what pushes him over the brink. I don't even want to think about where the money's going to come from.

Flashback—Mar. 1, 1994

I've been in LA for a week, dealing with the unexpected repercussions from a screening of Part 1 set up by Frank von Zerneck at a theater on the Universal lot. The original intent of the screening was simply to show the film to the LA cast, investors, and friends. Somehow, word got out about it and over 200 people came, including several independent distributors. The audience at that screening was so responsive that much of the dialogue could not be heard over the laughter.

Encouraged by this, I've been trying to set up meetings with people to finance the film as a feature. I've finished Part 3, which ends the film and incorporates all of the original actors. All I need is for someone to come in quickly with the money so I can make the film. The longer it takes, the harder it is to maintain the availability of a very large cast, specifically Steve and Dermot, who both have projects coming up immediately.

This anxiety is killing me. I've offered worldwide rights to every independent company I know. I started asking for $500,000, thinking it was about the least I could finish the film for. Yesterday I had a lunch meeting with Cy Bromitch, an Acquisitions Exec at a huge studio looking to get into low-budget films. Cy loved both the short and the new script.

"I love it," Cy said. "It's fresh, it's hip, it's funny. It's exactly the kind of thing we want to do."

"That's great!" I exclaimed, knowing they had a lot of money and $500,000 would be a drop in the bucket for them.

"And you know, $500,000 is just a drop in the bucket for us," Cy continued. "In fact, I could write you a check right now." He smiled warmly at me and mimed reaching for his checkbook.

"Great!" I said.

"But, I won't," Cy went on, miming putting his checkbook back in his pocket. "We love it but we feel it's just too small for us. OK? No hard feelings?"

"No, no, I understand," I said, taking the cigar out of his mouth and miming sticking the burning end right in his ear. Cy laughed, which was great because I'd been so excited I'd forgotten Chapter 5 of Eating Crow, *"Humor and Violence at the Lunch Meeting," and I was afraid he might have misinterpreted my playfulness.*

Today I called Jerry Fapple, an Acquisitions Exec at a big independent distributor. He put me on hold as he tried to conference in his partner, Lisa Muffler. They both had been at the screening. As I waited for the call to click in, I quickly changed my asking price from $450,000 to $350,000.

"Hi, Tom," Lisa said, with all the warmth of a token clerk.

"Hello, Lisa; hi, Jerry," I said. "I understand you both saw my short film."

"Loved it," Jerry said. "Very funny."

"Very funny," Lisa stated.

"Well, good," I went on, "because the reason I'm calling is that I've written two more sections of it, making it a feature,

and all I need is $300,000 to finish it, for which you guys could own the entire thing."

"This is the short we saw?" Jerry asked with some confusion. "You made a feature out of it?"

"Yeah, it's called Living in Oblivion *now, Jerry, and I've made it into a feature," I said, trying to be really clear about this.*

"Oh, why'd you do that?" Jerry sighed painfully into the phone. "It was so good as a short."

His question completely floored me and I really didn't know how to answer him.

"Well, I think it's even better now," I said finally. "Maybe I could send you the script and you can see what I've done with it?"

"Send it," Lisa said and hung up.

"Yeah, OK, go ahead, send it to me," Jerry said, cautiously.

"Thanks, Jerry," I said. "And listen, I'm absolutely convinced I can finish this film for $250,000."

———◆———

Jan. 15, 1995

Got a fax yesterday from Jerry Fapple. It's the first I've heard from him since I sent him the completed *Living in Oblivion* script last year.

"Dear Tom, Congratulations on getting into Sundance. Lisa and I would like to see your film ASPCA so we can ascertain if our company should make a preemptive, pre-Festival acquisition. Great talking to you a year and a half ago. Your pal, Jer Fapple."

I called Marcus and told him about Jerry's fax. He said he'd gotten one, too. Nevertheless, we decided to stick to our game plan and not show the film to any distributors till we get to Sundance.

It's a rather dreary Sunday in New York. I've got kind of a hangover. Had dinner last night with Camilla Toniolo, the editor of *Living in Oblivion*. Stu Wechner was there, another director whose film she'd cut. His film also had an unsuccessful release by a big independent distributor.

"Hey, don't get me started," Stu said immediately, even though no one had asked him to start anything. He then spent the next 2½ hours reliving for us every one of his nightmarish experiences with his distributor and the subsequent failure of his film. While some of his stories were told with a self-deprecating humor and were actually kind of funny, it was essentially a one-man show starring Stu and his bitterness. Ultimately, the way he had become fixated on his disappointment was very depressing and a little annoying. Just as I was about to punch him, he started crying.

It's such a brutal business. The feelings of bitterness and disappointment that come from failure are completely understandable, but completely unacceptable. No one wants to hear it. So, what do you do with these feelings? How do you resolve the frustration you feel when you see a film, no better or worse than your own, heralded by the press and ushered joyously into the golden arena of acceptance? How do you stay optimistic when you see a director, no better or worse than yourself, gain international recognition as a "film artist" and move on to other films while you struggle simply to pay the rent? How do you find the impulse to write another script and start down the twisted road of making another film when you feel no one is interested, no one understands, and no one cares if you give it all up tomorrow?

I don't know. The strangest irony for me is that *Living in Oblivion* came directly out of my own disappointment and somehow saved me from it.

---◆---

Jan. 18, 1995

It is 7:15 P.M. I am now at the *Living in Oblivion* Press Screening at Magno. I've decided to forgo the pleasure of watching the film with a room full of critics, and I'm sitting in the lobby just outside the theater, waiting to deliver the color

xerox posters to Marcus. He's leaving for Sundance early tomorrow morning and will put them up with Mike and Hilary
before I get there.

The film is nearing the end, where the crew is about to record 30 seconds of room tone. The projectionist's door is open
and the volume for his room speaker is turned up very loud.
The dialogue is blasting out of the waiting room and echoing
down the hallway, making everything sound forced and un-
natural. I keep fighting the impulse to get up and ask the projectionist to turn the sound down. For some reason the movie
seems absolutely defenseless at this moment.

The fact that it has managed to avoid disaster in the most
miraculous ways has prompted me to believe that it is blessed;
that nothing can hurt it. But just beneath that feeling is the
memory of every single rejection and dismissal *Johnny Suede*
encountered, fueling a fear that this film too will be ignored
and sink quickly into oblivion.

10:30 P.M. I am now at home. I was interrupted as I was
writing several hours ago by sudden applause coming from
behind the doors of the screening room. A moment later Marcus rushed out and told me quickly it was the best screening
of the film we've had. I met a few journalists, several of whom
expressed their positive reactions. Urman told me finally that
Janet Maslin did not attend and most likely will not see the
film until Sundance, which only means this particular anxiety
has now been postponed. I went across the street with Marcus, Mike, and Hilary for a much needed farewell drink with
my three producers.

Flashback—Mar. 1994

*I'm sitting here a little stupefied. We've got the money. Two
days ago I was just lying around, waiting for the phone to
ring when to my great surprise, it actually did. It was Floyd
Beamon, an extremely wealthy kid with $3 million who wants
to get into producing. One of my agents had invited him to the*

LA screening of Part 1, which interested him enough to offer me $300,000 for the worldwide rights. He was calling to confirm that he wanted to finance the feature version of the film.

"And listen," Beamon stated emphatically over the phone, "I'm not a hands-off kind of guy. I'm into this for my own chops; I want this film to put me on the map as a producer. I'll give you all the money but I'm telling you right now, I want stars in this. I'm going to be on the set every day; I'm going to be in the editing room every day. I'm going to be involved in every creative decision from casting to choosing the Festivals we'll go to. OK? That's the way it's going to be."

By this time, I had no options. Buscemi had a film offer pending that would make him unavailable for a year and the anxiety of losing him was driving me insane.

"OK, Floyd," I said with as much enthusiasm as I could muster. Beamon went on quickly to give me my flight information (he wanted me to sign the contract in LA, in person). Just then, my call waiting clicked in. It was Mike Griffiths, Hilary's husband, Speedo, the Soundman from Part 1.

"What's up, Mike?" I said quickly, knowing Floyd was waiting on the other line.

"Hilary and I were wondering," Mike began hesitantly, "if you would consider letting us put up the money for the rest of the film."

"Mike, come on," I snapped. "We're not talking about $20,000 here."

"I know," Mike said. "We want to put up the full $500,000."

I almost fell out of my chair. I managed to get back on the line with Floyd, and to his somewhat shocked surprise, told him I had a better offer and the deal was off.

The offer from Mike and Hilary is absolutely genuine. A deal memo has already been drawn up and we're to start pre-production in April. Miraculously, we'll be able to finish the film exactly the way we started it—with no outside interference and with no one to answer to but ourselves. My producers are not only my good friends, but two of my actors. If they give me any trouble I'll just cut their parts.

◆

Jan. 19, 1995

Buscemi called this morning with the great news that he'll be coming to Sundance after all. He'll arrive on the 25th and stay through the big screening on the 28th.

I got a call from L. M. Kit Carson, who'd been at the Press Screening. We met at the Sundance Director's Lab in 1991 and have become friends. He was one of the few advisers there who gave me detailed, constructive criticism on the screenplay for *Johnny Suede*. I was happy to hear he liked *Living in Oblivion*. He said the loopy, acerbic satire reminded him of Evelyn Waugh and James Thurber. He went on to say the film was "brave" but he said it with a hint of caution.

"What do you mean by 'brave'?" I asked.

"You're going to get some flak for it," he said. "You're saying things about filmmaking that no one's said before; that no one's supposed to say."

"Like what?"

"Like debunking the myth of the omnipotent director, Tom. Some people might get angry about that."

"You're right," I said. "All the people that think the director should only be seen brooding in half-shadow, with a cigarette hanging from his lip."

Flashback—Apr. 22, 1994

Today I auditioned three actors for the part of Tito, the Angry Dwarf. The first two had trouble getting to the rage I was looking for, so I asked them to come up with something from their own lives that might motivate them.

"What would make you angry right now?" I asked one guy.

He thought for a moment and said, "Try patting me on the head."

The other guy said he'd been on the subway, coming to the audition, and six high-school kids had gathered around him in a circle, snickering and talking in munchkin voices. Both

*actors startled me when they left, by thanking me for writing
a part like this.*

*The last guy I saw was Peter Dinklage. He needed no coax-
ing. His audition (the scene in which Tito ridicules Nick for
putting a dwarf in a dream sequence) was a jagged blend of
anger and hilarious bombast. He'd majored in theater at Ben-
nington and the imperious twist this added gave his Tito the
crucial human edge I was looking for. I gave him the part immediately. Ellen Lutter, our costume designer, was particularly happy about this. We start shooting in four days and she
still has to make Tito's blue tuxedo.*

*Came home and had a call from Brad Pitt. He's passing on
the Chad Palomino part. He says he wants to do it and I believe him. He genuinely sees the humor in the part. But he's
got a schedule conflict due to publicity requirements for* Leg-
ends of the Fall. *I immediately called James Legros and gave
him the part. We are now completely cast.*

---◆---

Jan. 20, 1995

Met with a guy today named Vic Merlot. He's a young kid,
about twenty, with a little goatee and big cigar. He's
written his first script, called *Hurt Me Tender,* which he wants
me to direct.

"You'll like it," he said. "It's got the same kind of humor as
Johnny Suede. It's about this really good-looking guy; right
now he's a serial killer but we could make him a rapist if you
want. He's hip, he's cool—Brad Pitt could really smoke the
role; or Quentin Tarantino."

"Do you have the money yet?" I asked.

"No," Vic said, "but I thought with you attached, maybe we
could get it to Brad and then the money will just come flying
in. Right? Isn't that the way you made *Suede?*"

"Actually, no," I said. "Brad wasn't a star when I cast him
and I spent four years trying to raise the money."

"Great, do you want me to call him, or maybe it should be
you?" Vic said eagerly.

"You know what, Vic?" I said, "I'm starting to get the feeling you're just using me to get to Brad. Now don't take this funny, but your pushy desperation is just about making me want to puke."

I didn't say that, even though I was feeling a little sick. That was probably from Vic's cigar. Instead, I remembered one of the shortest chapters of *Eating Crow*: "Channeling Anger into Compassion," and realizing Vic was just a kid trying to make a movie, like everybody else. I wished him luck, and said good-bye.

On my way home I stopped at the bank and took out $300 cash to bring to Sundance for food and expenses. My balance is now $3,700. I called Kelly Gordon at the Hirshhorn Museum in DC and asked her if she could advance me the $1,200 before screening *Living in Oblivion* there in March.

She apologized and said, "Since we're not screening the film for three months, I don't quite see how that would be possible."

The first Sundance screening of *Living in Oblivion* is at 9:00 P.M., Mountain Time, six hours from now. Marcus said he'll call me as soon as he wakes up tomorrow and give me the reaction.

Flashback—July 3, 1994

Camilla Toniolo and I have almost finished the rough cut of the film. Today I was in the editing room, staring at a shot of Steve Buscemi on the screen, and I was struck by a sudden sense of disbelief. It seemed only days ago that Catherine Keener had come up to me on the set of Part 1, and said, "You should make a feature out of this."

I was convinced then it was impossible. And now, eight months later, I was cutting one of the final scenes in the film, where Steve accepts his Golden Apple for Best Film Ever Made by a Human Being.

We shot Parts 2 and 3 in fifteen days at the beginning of May. This time everyone got paid and we shot 35mm. Most of the crew returned, as well as all of the cast. Once again every-one from LA paid their own way to NY and put themselves up.

I was relieved to feel the atmosphere of concentrated care-lessness return to the set after an eight-month hiatus. Once again, everyone seemed liberated by the fact that there was nothing at stake; nothing driving us but the desire to keep ourselves entertained.

I don't think anybody was prepared for James Legros. The only thing I said to him about Chad Palomino was that there is no doubt in the guy's mind he is an acting genius. Legros dove headfirst into the part and wallowed in it like a pig in a mudhole.

The same willingness was evident in all the actors. It amazes me that, with the exception of Peter Dinklage, no one auditioned for their parts. Danielle von Zerneck got the part of Wanda, the Assistant Director, due to the fact that she put up some money and she lived just down the street from Cath-erine and Dermot. Normally, she's cast in shy, ingenue roles. Any hesitation I had as to whether she was tough enough for the part disappeared the moment she barked to the fumbling crew, "Can we get a motherfucking frame line please?!!"

It also amazes me that out of fourteen actors, I never en-countered a single ego problem. In fact, I mostly had to con-tend with the opposite. We were filming a scene at the end of Part 2, where Steve and Catherine finally profess their love for each other and move into a beautiful, delicate kiss. The scene was exquisite. Afterwards, I noticed Steve moping in the shadows. I went up to him and said, "Hey, Steve. What's the matter?"

"It's this movie, Tom. I can't tell you how much it means to me."

"Come on. I'm just glad we could work together."

"No, you don't understand," he said with a sad smile. "Do you realize this is the first time in my career that I've kissed a woman on screen?"

* * *

There were some pretty hairy moments, though. One day stands out as the most agonizing one I've ever spent on a set. We were shooting the scene where Rica Martens, reappearing as Steve's slightly loony mother, walks into the shot Steve has been trying to get all day, and inadvertently saves it. I had written a long dialogue scene for this, but the moment Catherine, Rica, and I started rehearsing, I knew it didn't work. Nonetheless, due to the pressing schedule and the fact that I had no idea what else to do, we shot the scene.

It was pretty bad; not the acting, but the scene itself. What was most agonizing was knowing without a doubt, that the failure of this scene would cripple the entire film. I got home after midnight, too exhausted to do anything but go to sleep. But, sometime during the night I woke with a little hint of an idea. I got up and rewrote the scene, removing all the dialogue and essentially reducing the entire scene to one action: Cora walking in with the apple and performing the scene as she had seen Tito doing it.

We found some time the next day and shot the revised version and this is the scene that ended up in the film. I've destroyed all evidence of the original.

———◆———

Jan. 21, 1995

Fell asleep around 1:00 A.M., with the help of Stolichnya. Woke up around 4:00 A.M. Finally, at around 4:30, I got up and checked my machine to see if Marcus had called.

There was a message, but it was from Bobbi Thompson, my agent at William Morris. She'd called to tell me the first screening at Sundance had gone well. I went back to bed and finally fell asleep around 6:30.

At 11:00 A.M. Marcus called from Sundance. He said, "Tom, I've put just about every drug known to man in my body over the last thirty years but nothing comes close to what it felt like sitting through the screening last night."

As he went on with a fevered rush I've never heard in him

before, I listened to his words with a strange detachment, as if they were coming from someone's television in an apartment three floors down. He couldn't talk long because he had to run to a meeting with Bingham Ray from October Films, one of the four serious contenders for a US sale.

As soon as he hung up, a French distributor called from Sundance, wanting to set up a meeting. Joe Spaniel, from Artistic Artists called. Dermot called; I told him the news. Danielle called; I told her. Catherine called; I told her. Finally, to get away from the phone, I went with Jim Farmer (my composer) down to the Film Forum to see *Faster, Pussycat! Kill! Kill!*

Jan. 22, 1995

Was awake most of the night. Got up around 6:00 A.M. and basically spent the entire day in my pajamas, watching TV and falling asleep on the couch. The plane leaves tomorrow at noon. We're due to arrive in Park City around 8:00 P.M.

Am I nervous? The fact that I'm sleeping about two hours a night might answer that question. If we don't pick up a US distributor at Sundance it'll be almost impossible to get one afterwards. If we don't sell this film, the chances of me making another one will be pretty slim.

Flashback—Sept. 26, 1994

We screened the film today for the Sundance selection committee. Geoff Gilmore, the Festival Director, was there, along with John Cooper and Christian Gaines, the Festival's other two programmers. Not wanting them to view the film on videotape, I set up the screening while they were all in town for the annual Independent Feature Project.

The screening was in the same room at Magno where Richard Peña from the New York Film Festival had viewed the film two months earlier. This time, however, the place was packed.

I ran into Ulrich Gregor yesterday at the IFP and invited him. He's the Director of the Forum section of the Berlin Film Festival, which would be a great place to premiere the film in Europe. To my amazement he showed up. Two representatives came from the Rotterdam Film Festival. John Turturro and his wife Kathy came. I've been courting Turturro for over a year to play the lead in Box of Moonlight *and I wanted him to see this movie. Nonetheless, we all knew the sole purpose of the screening was to try and get into Sundance.*

I was somewhat reassured by the fact that we were showing a finished print that looked beautiful and included, for the first time, a 35mm blowup of Part 1. However, just before the film started, I suddenly realized it was only one of hundreds of movies Sundance was looking at. My experience with Johnny Suede *and festivals taught me there is literally no logic to what gets accepted and what doesn't. The rejection by the New York Film Festival reminded me there was a very real possibility Sundance might not take the film at all.*

After the screening, I stood around for a while talking to Turturro and some friends. I saw Gilmore and thanked him for coming. He said he liked the film, particularly the emotion underlying the humor. Then he said he wanted the film for Sundance. A moment later, Ulrich Gregor invited us to Berlin and just before I left, we received an invitation to Rotterdam as well.

──────◆──────

Jan. 23, 1995

Sitting on the plane at La Guardia writing this. 1:00 P.M. Just now taxiing out of the gate. I'm in the middle of three tight, cramped seats. Jane is on one side, on the other an old guy in a bright red sweater whose elbow is jammed so firmly into my ribs, it hurts when I breathe. Nothing like the intimacy of economy class.

Phone rang last night around 10:00 P.M. It was Marcus reporting from Sundance that the second screening had gone equally well. He said people were applauding between the acts, particularly when Rica walks in with the apple and saves the scene. Most of the distributors' second-tier buyers have seen the film and expressed interest in acquiring it.

Just before we left for the airport, Catherine Keener called from LA. It was only 6:00 A.M. there so I knew something was up. She told me a friend of Brad's had been at the Press Screening Wednesday and he had called Brad, asking him if he was still friends with the director (me). Apparently, this guy decided the character of Chad Palomino was a sarcastic dig at Brad. Catherine called to remind me to make it clear to the press that we'd offered Brad the part and it was not a caricature of him.

11:59 P.M. The Yarrow Hotel.

The plane landed in Salt Lake around 6:00 P.M. The Festival provided a shuttle van for the 40-minute trip to Park City. Among the other passengers were two young, gay women, filmmakers from San Francisco, coming to support a friend who had a documentary in the festival. They were crashing with this friend and had brought broccoli, spinach, and home-made tortellini in their backpacks. They gave me their number and said we could come over and use their jacuzzi any time.

The driver was a Salt Lake resident, going to college at Brigham Young University. He was majoring in Recreation and Leisure Time.

Checked into the hotel then met with Mark Urman, our publicist from DDA. He had a press schedule for me, which has interviews starting at tomorrow at 9:00 A.M. and ending at 6:30 P.M. At around 8:00 P.M., we hooked up with Marcus, Michael, and Hilary who filled me in. They had just come from a three-hour meeting with a foreign sales company called Summit, who wanted to handle all international sales, excluding North America. Although their first offer was low ($350,000), they quickly rose to $750,000 with a good back-end deal in which we all would share in the profits from sales to individual countries. Marcus feels strongly we should go with them.

In addition, Marcus said all the domestic distributors were sending their main buyers to the next screening Wednesday morning. Miramax has confirmed that Harvey Weinstein will be at that screening and has asked us not to accept any offers until he has seen it.

Later, we went to a party for *Search and Destroy*. John Turturro, who was in the film, had asked me to look him up. The party was in what looked like a three-story bar/stable/chalet at the end of Main Street. Just inside the door I ran into Turturro and his wife Kathy. I told him things were looking good for *Box of Moonlight*, especially in light of the positive attention *Living in Oblivion* was getting. He was in a great mood and appeared genuinely optimistic about his schedule. I hope to christ the *Box of Moonlight* deal comes together quickly. He would be brilliant in the part.

He and Kathy left quickly afterwards. We went upstairs and stood around with our coats on, breathing third-hand smoke. Norbert Beltcher, a local Festival Coordinator, came up and introduced himself. He leaned close to my ear and whispered, "The buzz on your film is swelling. The tide is turning in your favor; look for the Audience Award."

On the street a moment later, we ran into Geoff Gilmore, the Festival Director. He welcomed us to Sundance then stopped suddenly and looked over my shoulder.

"Hold on a second, Bob's coming up the street."

"Bob?" I said.

"Redford," he said. "He wants to see you again."

Like we were old friends; like we had gone to high school together. Fact is, I had never met the guy. A moment later I heard Gilmore exclaim, "Bob! Bob! Come here a second; here's Tom DiCillo."

I turned to see Redford coming toward me, followed by a group of fifteen people which was headed by a woman who, even in the dark, looked like she was in a very bad mood. In a daze I shook Redford's offered hand.

"Good to see you again," he said. "I've heard great things about your film."

I thanked him and congratulated him on *Quiz Show*, particularly his work with Turturro on Stempel's character. We stood chatting for a few moments with me feeling increasingly uncomfortable. It wasn't talking to "Robert Redford," it was the group behind him, all staring at me in sullen suspicion, especially the woman in the bad mood. Suddenly she darted between us and announced, "Are we cold enough yet?!"

I started to walk away with Redford following me. He said he wanted to get together while I was at Sundance. Just as I was convinced he was either bullshitting or totally drunk, he winked at me and said, "I'm serious; we'll get together and share a few war stories about *Johnny Suede* and *A River Runs Through It*."

———◆———

Jan. 24, 1995

Started my interviews at 9:00 A.M. with John Anderson from *New York Newsday*. Did a radio interview with David D'Arcy from NPR and then a grueling hour with a woman from *The San Antone Weekly*. She spent the first half hour talking about the significance of my parents' birthplace and the second talking about Tarantino.

At one point I said, "Tarantino may have just made Jim Jarmusch obsolete. He's made the first independent art film embraced by middle America that's about to gross over $100 million."

The woman looked at me quizzically and asked, "Jarmusch? Is he that Hungarian filmmaker?"

I was alarmed to hear several reporters ask about the Brad Pitt "rumor." I had to go into detail with them all and explain why it is so obviously untrue. Kathleen McInnis at *Moviemaker* asked if there was one question I found most journalists never asked.

I said, "Yeah, they never ask about the Black Period; that

endless stretch of time in between making films. Most journalists seem to think filmmakers just yawn and fart out their
next film whenever they have nothing else to do. No one seems
to have any idea of the years of sacrifice and the hundreds of
Nos you hear before you get the chance to run one foot of film
through the camera."

Most of the interviews took place at a restaurant called the
Claimjumper on Main Street. During a break, I ran into Heidi
and Ingmar from PAP Entertainment. Ingmar wanted to
know how much we are asking for the film, so he could "ac-
cess" competitive bids. Somewhat concerned that he was confused as to who was representing the film, I said he should
talk to Marcus before he accessed anything. Then he told me
he wanted to set up a meeting for me with Swifty Chesner, a
wealthy manager who was getting into producing. Ingmar has
a way of looking at you, staring persistently at a point right
between your eyes like a dog begging for a piece of bologna. It
makes you want to either say "yes" or smack his nose. However, hearing Heidi echo her husband's claim that this Swifty
guy had a lot of money and was very excited about meeting
me, I agreed to have breakfast with them.

After my last interview, Jane, Bobbi Thompson, and I went
to a Filmmaker's Dinner sponsored by Royalty, one of the
smaller US distributors at Sundance. I spoke to a couple of
people I knew: Tom Noonan and his wife Karen Young, who
were sitting with Michael Almereyda. Noonan's film *The Wife*
and Almereyda's film *Nadja* are also in the competition.

For dinner, however, I ended up at an almost empty table
sitting next to Rafe Snedding, one of Royalty's chief production execs. He seemed extremely ill at ease and kept half-
starting conversations with a pained expression on his face,
as if he was convinced (like me) that he belonged at a much
more interesting table.

It was pretty grueling. We were just about to leave when
Norbert Beltcher, the Festival Coordinator I'd met, slipped
into an empty seat beside me. He leaned closer to give me this
urgently whispered status report on Festival "buzz."

"OK, you're just about at the midpoint of the festival now.

You've got a lot of buzz, you and *Brothers McMullen*. Both of you have a really good shot at the Audience Award. But what you need to do right now is relax, sit back, and see what the audience is going to do; because it's midpoint now, a crucial time. The audience could swell or they could slip away from you; they could fade, pull back, then resurge onto another film. And then—you've lost them. Hey, it's been known to happen."

"Maybe I should go out and buy a cheerleader's outfit and hold some kind of pep rally for the film," I said, jokingly. I was quite alarmed when Beltcher did not laugh. His chilly silence prompted me to continue quickly, "Just kidding, Norbert. Thank you, that's very good advice; I'll try to remember it."

And I really did have to try, because for the life of me, I couldn't remember what the hell his advice had been. Mainly though, I was pissed off at myself for forgetting Chapter 9 of *Eating Crow*: "Offending Festival Coordinators: Your Film, Your Future and The Toilet Bowl."

Standing on Main Street a few minutes later, we ran into Catherine, Dermot, Danielle, and her husband James. They were on their way to a movie, so I filled them in quickly on what had been happening and made plans to meet them at the theater in the morning.

On the way back to the hotel I spotted Marcus trying to get into a crowded bar while talking on his cellular phone. He hung up long enough to tell me the Summit deal looked final. I said I wanted to meet Patrick Wachsburger before we signed anything and Marcus said he'd already set up a meeting for tomorrow. He still wanted to announce the deal right away, unofficially, to help stir confidence with domestic distributors.

————◆————

Jan. 25, 1995

Got to the theater at 9:45 A.M. and was surprised to see a line of people spilling out the door. The crowd, however, did little to relieve my anxiety. 10:20 in the morning didn't seem like an ideal time to screen a movie, especially with a theater filled largely with distributor decision makers. Michael Barker and Tom Bernard were there from Sony Classics. I saw Harvey Weinstein walk in. Tom Rothman was there, from his new company Fox Searchlight. I had known him since 1984 when he worked at Goldwyn. Bingham Ray from October, Rona Wallace from Goldwyn, and Ruth Vitale, Bob Aaronson's boss and the new head of Fine Line. I'm still scheduled to have a lunch meeting with Vitale in the next few days. I had originally intended to watch the film for the first time with a Festival audience but with this crowd I decided to just introduce the film and get the hell out.

I stood in the doorway of the theater with Catherine and Jane. Harvey walked by and we shook hands.

"I've heard great things about the film, Tom," he said. "Maybe I'll do the right thing by it this time."

"Well, I hope you like it, Harvey," was all I could think of saying with a burst of nervous laughter.

Tom Rothman came up and insisted we take no offers until after we met with him. He was the third person who'd heard we were close to selling foreign rights to Summit. At that point I was so tense I was having trouble breathing. People were knotted all around me, pushing, yelling, and trying to get in. A Mormon usher was grabbing people who'd already bought tickets, pulling them back into the lobby and telling them they couldn't get in.

After introducing the film, I went to a nearby coffee shop with Jane and Catherine. We talked for a while with Ira Schreck, a New York lawyer who'd been assisting in negotiations on the Summit deal. We were interrupted by Istvan Flurnik, a Russian producer who'd seen the film and urgently wanted to talk about his company producing my next one. Mainly though, he talked about his company, for 45 minutes. What made this particularly agonizing was the fact his breath smelled like fresh cat shit.

My relief when Flurnik left was short-lived; Ira Shreck suddenly stood up and went to the door.

"It's Harvey," Ira said. "He just walked out of the movie. I'll be right back."

While I waited for Ira to return I felt a cold dread rise in me. I knew instantly Harvey had passed on the film but that wasn't what bothered me. It was more the fear that once word got out he had passed, it would weaken the film in the eyes of all the other distributors. I envisioned five giant rats stumbling over themselves in their haste to get off the sinking ship. A moment later Ira came back in.

"He passed. He said it's not for him." Seeing my distress he went on, "Come on, it's the best thing for you. Now you can concentrate on selling it to the people you really want, and who really want the film. No one's going to pull out. The only thing that will happen is your price will go down because you've just lost your biggest bidder."

At 1:30 P.M. we had a meeting with Bingham Ray from October. To my relief, Bingham spoke warmly about the film and stated that he wanted to buy it. He could only offer $300,000, but I liked his plan to open the film as soon as possible, sometime during the summer. I left the meeting feeling somewhat disappointed in the price but impressed with Bingham and confident a sale to October would be good for the film.

Had to run to make a 2:00 P.M. press conference for all the directors with films in the Dramatic Competition. I saw one or two people I knew: Tom Noonan, Michael Almereyda, Nick Gomez—most were complete strangers. It was the first time all the directors had been together in the same room at the Festival.

The conference was dominated by one journalist in the front row whose questions were more declarations of his own pet theories, such as, "Sundance has become commercialized and you as filmmakers are responsible."

Tom Noonan responded. "Commercialized?" he said, "I don't know what you're talking about. I don't think there's anybody in this room who made their movie hoping no one would see it."

I didn't say too much because I was too busy figuring out how to pocket the quarter I'd spotted on the carpet a few feet away. At one point this same journalist asked us all to say who had inspired us to keep going in times of desperation.

I said, "Quentin Tarantino," which prompted some nervous

laughter. Nick Gomez said, "Parker Posey," the actress star-ring in *Party Girl* who had been prancing around the Festival in multicolored miniskirts.

Went back to the Claimjumper afterwards and did a few inter-views until 5:30. Had several more insistent queries about the Brad Pitt rumor. "Is it true Chad Palomino is Brad Pitt?" No matter how strongly I deny it, the distracted look in their eyes while I'm talking tells me they've already written the story.

A half hour later, in a pool hall bar, we had our first meeting with Tom Bernard and Michael Barker from Sony Classics. The jukebox was blasting some local bar band's version of "Foxy Lady," and even though we were the only ones in the place, the only way we could get them to turn the shit down was by buying bar memberships for all of us; which, by the way, is the only way you can get a drink in a bar in Utah.

I was immediately impressed by Barker's and Bernard's en-thusiasm for the film. They talked about the emotional under-current supporting the humor. They referred to specific scenes and they knew most of the actors by name. I asked when they were thinking of releasing it and like Bingham, they said summer. I was further impressed to learn they were releasing Todd Haynes's *Safe*, Hal Hartley's *Amateur*, and Terry Zwi-goff's *Crumb*. They both seemed accessible, smart, and very motivated.

They offered us $500,000. Now we have significant offers from two respected distributors, October and Sony Classics. Still pending is a meeting tomorrow with Tom Rothman who "loves" the movie and wants to make an offer. Meanwhile, Goldwyn and Fine Line are still expressing interest.

Had dinner with Dermot, Jane, Danielle, and James Fearn-ley. Catherine was asleep. It snowed all during dinner. After-wards in the parking lot Fearnley started a half hour snowball fight by throwing a snowball across the street at a group of people waiting quietly for a bus.

—— ◆ ——

Jan. 26, 1995

I did some press until 12:30 P.M. then had a break. Mark Urman suggested we drop by a lunch *The New York Times* was hosting. He pointed out Bernard Weinraub from *The Times* and reminded me I had an interview scheduled with him for tomorrow. Urman walked off and a moment later came rushing back.

"Weinraub has to cancel his interview with you tomorrow but he wants to do it right now, while he's talking to Janet Maslin!"

"Has she seen the film?"

"No."

"Listen," I said, "I don't feel comfortable talking to the chief *Times* film critic about a film she hasn't seen yet."

"Tom, you've got to do this," Urman said. "They're leaving in five minutes."

So I went over, fighting the apprehension that increased with each step. All I could think of was Vincent Canby's dismissive review of *Johnny Suede* in *The New York Times*, even though that was three years ago and he no longer wrote film reviews.

Weinraub's relaxed and friendly demeanor put me somewhat at ease. He reminded me of an uncle of mine who was very adept at playing the horses. He told Maslin she should definitely see the movie. She was quietly courteous and if anything, seemed a little shy. The whole interview lasted about two minutes. Weinraub took a few notes and Maslin said she would try to see the film at its last screening Friday afternoon.

Urman came rushing up afterwards wanting to know how it went. I said, "I have no idea."

At 2:00 P.M. I met Marcus and Bobbi on Main Street in front of the deli where our meeting with Rothman was to take place. Marcus said he'd already spoken to Rothman that morning and he was coming to make an offer. Then Marcus gave me some bad news. Fine Line and Goldwyn had passed, both dismissing the film as "too inside Hollywood."

"What do you mean 'inside Hollywood'?" I asked. "It's obviously a New York low-budget crew, shooting in New York City, with no agents, no producers, no suits; in fact there isn't a single reference to Hollywood in the entire film. What are they talking about?!"

No one even bothered to answer my question. After ten minutes of waiting, Bobbi and I went inside to get something to eat. While I was sitting there, some guy came running up to me.

"Hey Tom! Vic Merlot!"

"Hey Vic, how are you? What are you doing here?"

"I'm here with *Hurt Me Tender*, man. I just got a deal; $6 million. I'm directing it myself. We just made an offer to Uma Thurman for the lead."

"The rapist/serial killer? I thought you wanted Brad or Quentin for that?" I asked.

"No, I changed it to a girl. See that? It's a whole new spin on the genre. It's fresh now, right?"

"No, yeah. It sounds good. Congratulations."

"Thanks!" Vic yelled. "Got to run."

Vic ran out and twenty minutes later Rothman and Marcus came rushing in. Rothman shook my hand and sat down.

"Tom, I loved your movie," he said. "It's fresh, it's funny, it's got a great spirit to it. Your talent as a director is without question. Your cast is incredible. I loved Buscemi; I think he's definitely Oscar material. Catherine Keener, James Legros—I loved them all. I loved your movie."

"That's great, Tom," I said. "I'm glad to hear it."

Rothman went on. "But I'm going to pass."

I looked over at Marcus in surprise. He just stared at me as Rothman explained.

"You see, my company is new, Tom. We're just starting out. I would need to release your film immediately, beginning of summer at the latest, and we are completely unprepared to do that. It would be bad for you. And after what you went through with *Johnny Suede*, I don't want to be responsible for you having another movie that doesn't get seen. Because people should see this movie, Tom, and they will. I know they will. But I just can't get it ready in time."

Two minutes later we shook hands and he left.

"I'm just as shocked and surprised as everyone else is, but it makes sense to me," Marcus said a moment later.

"I'm still a little confused," I said.

"So am I," said Bobbi.

Still, Fox/Searchlight is now out. This leaves only October and Sony.

After the meeting, Marcus and I drove into the mountains for a 6:30 P.M. meeting with Patrick Wachsburger, the President of Summit. The drive provided us our first real chance to talk since my arrival. Marcus had been calling Sony all day, trying to get them to raise their offer of $500,000. They wouldn't budge.

"Should we go back to October and see if Bingham will match Sony's offer?" I asked.

"I already called Bingham," Marcus said. "He can't go any higher than $300,000."

We drove in silence for a while. "It's pretty obvious, isn't it?" Marcus said a moment later.

"What?" I asked.

"That it's going to be Sony," Marcus said.

We drove deeper into the canyon through thick, rapidly falling snowflakes. Outside Wachsburger's rented condo we met Mike and Hilary who'd been waiting for us. The place was gigantic, with massive wooden foundations spreading up the face of a cliff. Inside, we found Wachsburger on the phone and another man and woman on other phones. A moment after we sat down, the woman came over with a bottle of wine and poured us all a glass, all except Mike who does not drink.

My first impression of Wachsburger was that he was a smooth operator—smart and wily. This was Summit's first foray into the world of low-budget independent film. Mainly they were known for selling big Hollywood commercial films.

However, the more we talked the more I was impressed with Wachsburger. He seemed sincerely interested in finding the right independent distributors for the film and in getting the film seen by the largest audience.

Things hit a sudden snag when Wachsburger described how the film would be dubbed in each territory. I freaked out, horrified at the thought of disembodied foreign voices replacing all the distinctively expressive vocal work of my actors. Wachsburger said there would, of course, be one subtitled print in each major city but the problem was even major cities only had one or two theaters that showed subtitled prints. No distributor would buy the film if they knew they could only show it in one theater. I asked him to find out if Jarmusch's movies are dubbed, also Tarantino's, Campion's, and Gus Van Sandt's.

At that point Wachsburger made a toast to the film. We all raised our glasses, including Mike whose glass was empty. Wachsburger paused, then suddenly exclaimed, "You can't drink from an empty glass!"

The gravity with which he said this made it sound like a proclamation from a Buddhist monk. While he went into the kitchen to put water in Mike's glass, I called out to him, "They should put that in all the fortune cookies in New York."

"What?" Wachsburger said, frowning in mild confusion.

"You Can't Drink From an Empty Glass," I said.

We left and drove quickly to the Prospector Hotel for a group interview for Showtime. They put Dermot and me next to each other on a big couch, with Catherine and Danielle beside us. The woman doing the interview asked us each to say what *Living in Oblivion* meant to us personally. The responses from Dermot, Catherine, and Danielle were wry, eloquent, and hilarious. All I could think of saying was, "It means having the chance to make a movie the way I wanted to, without ever once having to get down on my knees."

Hilary and Mike took us all out to dinner afterwards. It was great having everybody together. The only one missing was Buscemi, due to arrive tomorrow morning. Hilary made a speech and started crying after her first word. Had a half-assed snowball fight in the parking lot after, then went back to the hotel.

Two messages were waiting for me when I got in. One was from Wendy Keys at The New Directors Series in NY. She was asking again if her committee could look at the film. I still don't know if I should let New Directors be the New York premiere of the film. A bad review from *The New York Times* before the film is officially released would be disastrous.

The other message was an automated female voice from my bank informing me that, "There are no funds, I repeat, no funds in your checking account. You have no funds to cover check number 7221."

———◆———

Jan. 27, 1995

Dragged myself to the breakfast meeting at the Yarrow Hotel with Ingmar and Heidi from PAP Entertainment, and their manager contact, Swifty Chesner. I was in a foul mood, probably hungover, but definitely not thrilled I'd allowed myself to be talked into this meeting. My one consolation was that they were paying for the breakfast. My $300 expense money is now down to around $50.

I tried to concentrate on what Heidi had reiterated just before Swifty showed up: "This man has a lot of money and a lot of Hollywood connections. He wants to help you make your next film (*The Real Blonde*). So, don't blow it."

But for some reason, everything I'd learned from *Eating Crow* was just flying out the window. Swifty started off well by saying, "No matter what your Little Team has done for you, they have not capitalized on *Living in Oblivion* the way I would have. I'd have at least three or four studio deals set up for you now."

"That's interesting, Swifty," I said. "But without my 'little' team this movie would never have gotten made. And if I hadn't made the movie I'm wondering if you and I would even be talking right now. You know what I'm saying?"

This prompted a long moment of silence until Heidi jumped in and brought up *The Real Blonde*. She thought Swifty would be the perfect person to help me set up the financing, with PAP attached as producers. Swifty began listing the star actors he managed. Suddenly Heidi giggled and said, "With producers like me and Ingmar, it seems destined we should be producing a script called *The Real Blonde*."

"Why?" I asked.

"'Cause we're both blonde," Heidi said.

"Well, you'd have to prove it," I heard myself say.

"That could be arranged!" said Heidi, prompting a suggestive chortle from Ingmar that made me a little nervous they were both going to show me the evidence right there at the table.

Fortunately, the meeting ended shortly afterwards and I left, promising them all that I would get back to them.

At 2:30 P.M. I went over to the Prospector Theater for the final screening of *Living in Oblivion*. A line of people on the waiting list was already stretching down the long corridor leading to the theater's entrance. Making my way through the crowd, I ran headfirst into Steve Buscemi coming the other way. He'd just arrived from Minneapolis and was rushing to an interview before the film started. We barely had time for a frantic greeting before his publicist pulled him away.

Marcus was jammed into the crowd at the door, dealing with people screaming for tickets. I pulled him aside and asked him what the progress was with the Sony offer.

"500,000," he said. "They won't budge. But it's a good deal. I think we should sign it."

"So do I," I said.

"Good," Marcus said. "I'll announce it right after the screening." Then some guy in a suit grabbed him.

"You got to let me in!" the guy yelled. "I am somebody!"

We moved into the theater, which was by now standing room only. As I waited with Marcus along the side wall, I suddenly noticed Janet Maslin sitting in the audience. Pointing her out to Marcus I said, "Well, this is it. Here comes our *Times* review."

Even above the noise of the crowd I heard Marcus groan, "Oh, God."

Just then Geoff Gilmore walked on stage and introduced me. I went up, said a few things about the film, then found a seat next to Jane and sat through the screening—my first one at Sundance. I broke out into a sweat immediately and didn't relax until the end of Part 1, when Steve wakes up. The audience applauded then, and again at the end of Part 2 when Catherine wakes up. They seemed thrilled and astonished that they'd been fooled twice. Cheers and applause followed Cora's (Rica Martens) saving the scene in Part 3. Rica's feisty looniness was a real crowd-pleaser, as was Dermot's goofy, ego-ridden Wolf.

When it was over I asked Marcus, Steve, Catherine, Dermot, Danielle, Kevin Corrigan, and Frank Prinzi (the DP) on stage for the discussion. The questions from the audience suggested they'd appreciated the film on several levels, which pleased me. No one brought up the Brad Pitt rumor, which pleased me even more. Marcus then made the official announcement the film had been sold domestically to Sony Classics and internationally to Summit.

William Morris had set up a cocktail party for the film in an adjacent room immediately after the screening. At one point I found myself jammed up against Brendan Lemon from *The New Yorker*. I was pleased to hear he liked the film, particularly Steve's performance. I was right in the middle of a sentence with him when a woman with a strange, pained look on her face suddenly interrupted me.

"I'm starting a fund to help directors whose first films bombed and went nowhere," she said, quite loudly. "Since *Johnny Suede* fits right into that category I thought you might like to make a donation."

"I'm sort of broke right now," I said, "but I will make a donation to tattoo a sign on your forehead that says, 'Forgive me, I'm just a little fucking stupid.'"

Just before I could say that, an Italian director introduced himself and offered his enthusiastic affection for the film as well as his assistance in helping us secure an Italian distributor. Then he tugged my arm and whispered, "Don't answer this right now but I would like you to consider selling me the rights to an Italian remake of your film."

"The film hasn't even opened in Italy," I said.

"I know, it is very premature, but I think I could make a very good Italian version of your film, with Italian actors—it would do really well in Italy."

I said, "Listen, I'm flattered, but I can tell you right now I don't want two versions of this film floating around the world. This is the film, and I want people to see it as I made it."

"I think maybe you are being a little hasty," he said. "I'll come back in a few minutes."

Moments later Marcus and I were interviewed by a guy from the *L.A. Times* who kept asking me for "poop." When I asked him what he meant he said, "You know, poop about distributors; poop on Sundance; things like that."

I told him one of the stories of me begging for money to finish the film. He wanted names.

"No," I said.

"Come on," he urged. "I want the poop; give me names."

"Why should I give you names?" I said. "You'll print them and everyone will think I'm whining to the press. I could alienate several major financing sources. You have nothing to lose. You'll just print your story about poop and then pick up your paycheck."

"You're no fun," he said. "You're afraid."

"You're right," I said. "I'm afraid you've been sniffing so hard for poop, you've worked your head right up your ass."

Marcus interjected before I could say that which was nice of him because I had completely forgotten Chapter 14 of *Eating Crow*, called "Journalists Could Be People Too."

Catherine's agent Jeanne invited all of us from *Living in Oblivion* to join her group for dinner. There were about fourteen of us in total. Just after we sat down, another group of fourteen from the same agency, approached the table with the maître d'. It seems this group had used the agency's reservation also. They wanted us to get up and let them have the table. Jeanne refused. A semifamous actress and a semifamous actor's wife headed this other group and their tone quickly became sullen and threatening. Finally the maître d' offered to set up a special table for them and the entire group shuffled off in sour reluctance.

Ten minutes later the semifamous actress and the semifamous actor's wife came back to the table, one of them clutching a pen and a piece of paper. They demanded Jeanne's name. Jeanne gave them her first name. They demanded her last.

Watching this pretty display of intraagency politics put me in a bad mood. We left quickly afterwards and went to a party for *Party Girl* in a bar up the street. The place was so crowded over a hundred people, including Party Girl herself, Parker Posey, were standing outside in the snow.

I ran into Bob Aaronson. It was the first time I'd seen him in person since the Christmas party where he had so vigorously pressed me to see the film. Now he was apologizing for Fine Line passing.

"No big deal," I said. "We're going with Sony."

He then informed me Ruth Vitale was cancelling her lunch meeting with me. At one point, I turned and found myself face to face with a guy who looked vaguely familiar.

It was Henri Brulee, a French producer who'd once been interested in financing *Box of Moonlight*. The last time I'd seen him was at a lunch meeting three years earlier. His parting words to me then were, "I loave this script. I will make it happen. We are in bees knees. I will call you tomorrow morning."

I never heard from the guy again. When I called his hotel, I was told he'd checked out and there was no message leaving a forwarding address. Now he was standing in front of me grinning.

"Ah, Tom. Good to see you!"

"Hello, Henri," I said. "I'm not sure, but weren't we going to have a phone call or something?"

Henri shrugged apologetically. "Ah, Tom. I am sorry. I am vary busy with a vary special project. Do you know Zjeem Keri?"

"Is that a card game?" I asked.

"No, Zjeem Keri," he said. *"The Mask, Ace Ventura . . ."*

"Oh, Jim Carrey," I said.

"Yes," Henri went on. "I am talking with his agent. We want him for the lead in *American Psycho*. You know this? Bread Yeast on Alice?"

"Brett Easton Ellis?"

"Yes. Genius book. Genius casting. Zjeem Keri in first serious role."

"That's a great idea," I said. "Good luck."

"Thank you, Tom. And good luck to you too on *Living in Bolivia*."

As Jane and I walked down Main Street to the hotel, I was reminded for some reason of something Fred Kareman, my acting teacher, had once said: "Most people in this business should be selling zippers on 7th Avenue."

---◆---

Jan. 28, 1995

I did a couple of final interviews in the morning then went to a meeting with Axle Films, another company that was interested in financing *Box of Moonlight*. Marcus and Bobbi accompanied me to the meeting with June Murley and Sissy Flotard, two Axle execs. They liked the script and were ready to finance it except for one "little issue." June finally told me what the "issue" was.

"Several women in our office object to the fact that Al (the lead character I want Turturro for) sleeps with a woman other than his wife."

Sissy then interjected helpfully, "Perhaps Al and this other woman could just cuddle all night instead."

I spent a few minutes explaining my intent with this script point and even suggested I would consider filming a scene at the end where Al might confess this "sin" to his wife. Then I realized what I was doing.

"You know what, June? Sissy? I don't think there is anything wrong or problematic with the script. In fact, I think it is absolutely fine that Al sleeps with this woman and frankly, it is also fine if he never tells his wife about it. I know I forget sometimes this country was founded by Puritans, but I still can't quite understand how it's OK to show a woman getting raped or hacked to death in a film but it is taboo to show two human beings sharing a brief moment of sensual joy."

"You're exactly right," said June. "We just acquired a brilliant script that progressively addresses this very issue. It's called *Hurt Me Tender* written by Vic Merlot and Uma Thurman is playing the lead."

The Closing Night Awards Ceremony was held later that night in a private indoor tennis club. Jane and I went with Catherine and Dermot, but due to Redford's presence, the security at the door was so intense we almost didn't get in. We found seats just off the right of the stage next to Steve Buscemi, and took turns sipping on the pint of vodka I'd snuck in. We'd just about finished it when Redford came out and started the Ceremony by giving a surprisingly moving and eloquent speech.

They gave out the Special Jury Prizes first, then to my complete surprise *Living in Oblivion* won the Screenwriting Award. The Audience Award went to *Picture Bride*, and a moment later the Grand Jury Prize went to *Brothers McMullen*.

I passed Norbert Beltcher leaving the hall and I assumed it was probably the vodka that made me ask him, "Hey Norbert, what the hell happened with the Audience Award? I thought you said it was going to either *Living in Oblivion* or *Brothers McMullen*?"

Beltcher shrugged it off. "*Picture Bride* came out of nowhere," he said. "They flourished in the middle lag period and edged you both out in the final stretch."

* * *

The Awards Party was so crowded we decided to skip it and go someplace else to eat. I was a little tired of talking to people and sick of talking about *Living in Oblivion*. Unfortunately all the restaurants along Main Street were closed. At 10:30 P.M. we were the only people on the street. Finally we found an all-night deli and sat down to a dinner of pizza and beer. Which actually worked out OK because it enabled me to buy a round of beers on the last of my expense money. Afterward we stood on the street and I said good-bye to my actors, producers, friends; this crazy group of people who had miraculously come together for the making of this film.

Later that night, Jane noticed me moping around the hotel room and asked me if I was disappointed.

I said, "I don't know, maybe; a little bit."

She said, "Well, then you're a fucking idiot. You accomplished everything you came here to do. You sold the film domestically to Sony Classics, internationally to Summit Entertainment, and on top of everything you got an award for something you worked really hard on."

I got in bed, started thinking about it and I realized she was right. Feeling somewhat better, I went to sleep. Sometime during the night a loud knocking at the door woke me up. I stumbled out of bed, wrapped a towel around me and opened the door. Geoff Gilmore, the director of the Sundance Film Festival, was standing there, surrounded by Whit Stillman, Samuel Jackson and the rest of the Jury. Behind them was a group of reporters with cameras.

"Sorry to wake you, Tom," Gilmore began. "But something kind of amazing has happened and we wanted to tell you immediately. The Jury made a mistake in its counting of the votes. It has now determined that *Living in Oblivion* is the new and official winner of the Audience Award, the Grand Jury Prize, and in an unprecedented achievement, every single award at the 1995 Sundance Film Festival."

In shock, I reached for the Golden Apple that Whit Stillman held out to me, and suddenly the towel dropped from around my waist. As I froze in the doorway, completely naked in front of nine startled and staring Jurors, an endless series of flashes burst from the reporters' cameras.

I suddenly awoke and found myself staring at the hotel alarm clock which read in large unblinking numbers: 4:30 A.M.

———◆———

In May 1994, *Living in Oblivion* was made into a feature film, starring the following actors:

Steve Buscemi	◆ Nick Reve
Catherine Keener	◆ Nicole
Dermot Mulroney	◆ Wolf
James Legros	◆ Chad Palomino
Danielle von Zerneck	◆ Wanda
Rica Martens	◆ Cora
Peter Dinklage	◆ Tito
Robert Wightman	◆ Bob, the Gaffer
Kevin Corrigan	◆ A.C.
Hilary Gilford	◆ Scriptgirl
Michael Griffiths	◆ Soundman
Matthew Grace	◆ Boomman
Tom Jarmusch	◆ Jeff, the Driver
Ryan Bowker	◆ Bert, the Clapper
Francesca diMauro	◆ Cybil, the Craft Servicer
Norman Field	◆ Lorde, the Make-up Artiste

The film won the Waldo Salt Screenwriting Award at the 1995 Sundance Film Festival. It opened the New Films, New Directors Series at the Museum of Modern Art and was an official selection at the Berlin Film Festival, the San Francisco Film Festival and the Seattle Film Festival. The film will be released domestically by Sony Pictures Classics. Summit Entertainment has sold the film throughout the world.

Living
in
Oblivion

The Original Screenplay

One

A battered 35mm movie camera stands alone on a wooden tripod surrounded by blackness. Opening credits begin. An almost imperceptible DOLLY in toward the movie camera. The dolly forward continues throughout the credits ending in an EXTREME CU of the camera's lens, filling the frame like a giant, glass full moon. Fade to BLACK.

Suddenly a door opens directly in front of the camera, wiping the lens and revealing the following scene in Black and White.

1. **EXT. STREET. NYC. NIGHT.**

A quiet, deserted industrial street. It is over an hour before dawn and the street is still cloaked in the heavy stillness of night.

In the weak light filtering out of their battered van, BERT and CYBIL—the Craft Service Managers, finish setting out breakfast supplies on a 6′ table. They work in almost complete silence, both nearly paralyzed with sleep. A cheap walkie-talkie, lying beside a paper plate of soggy Oreos, sputters and buzzes occasionally. Other items on the table include a mangled banana, seven grapes, and a box of chocolate covered donuts.

                    BERT

What time is it?

CYBIL

Four. Why?

BERT

This milk is bad.

CYBIL

(sniffs) When did you buy it?

BERT

Tuesday? I don't know. What's today?

CYBIL

Monday. (pause) There's a deli on Broadway.

BERT

Nothing closer?

CYBIL

Nothing that's open.

BERT

(sniffs the milk) Is it that bad?

CYBIL

I don't know. You're the one who said it was bad.

At that moment a large truck grinds around the corner and shudders to a stop in front of the building. Bert replaces the carton of milk neatly beside the orange juice.

2. **EXT. STREET. NYC. NIGHT. B/W**

Amid low, one-word greetings, the CREW tumbles out of the trucks and stands in a groggy cluster around the Craft

Service table. WOLF—the Cameraman, assumes a place of prominence. He wears a black leather coat, a black beret, and black leather half-fingered gloves.

WOLF

This is the worst fucking coffee I've had in my life.

CYBIL

Then don't drink it.

GAFFER

What're we doing today?

WOLF

(pulls out a wrinkled callsheet) "Interior. Living Room. Ellen talks to Mom."

AC

Any nudity?

CYBIL

Yeah, you have to take your fucking pants off.

AC

I'll do it. I like Ellen.

GAFFER

Yeah, she's a babe. She was the nurse in that Richard Gere movie.

BERT

I worked on that.

                              AC
The shower scene.

                             WOLF
Start with the 5K in the window. Run feeders for
three blonds into the living room.

                            GAFFER
Two people. Sitting? Standing?

                             WOLF
Who fuckin' knows?

                            GAFFER
(walks off) "Ellen talks to Mom."

3. INT. CAR. NIGHT. B/W.

NICOLE sits quietly in the back seat of a beat-up station
wagon. She glances out at the empty city moving past her
window and lets out a deep sigh.

JEFF, the young intern assigned as her driver, glances
into the rearview mirror.

                             JEFF
Tired?

                            NICOLE
No, I've been up since four. I've got a big scene
today and I'm kind of nervous.

                             JEFF
"Ellen talks to Mom."

NICOLE

Have you read the script?

JEFF

No. It's on the callsheet.

NICOLE

Oh. Well, it's pretty emotional. I tell my mother I never felt she really loved me.

JEFF

You're going to yell at each other?

NICOLE

I don't know. I'm just going to go with how I feel. Which is the scary part. I'm very close to this character.

JEFF

Problems with your own mom?

NICOLE

Yes. But she died before I, well before we could reconcile . . .

JEFF

You were great in that Richard Gere movie.

NICOLE

Thanks.

4. **EXT. RESIDENTIAL HOTEL. NIGHT. B/W.**

CU sidewalk. A pair of women's orthopedic shoes enter the frame and begin pacing.

Camera pans up to reveal CORA, a small woman in her early 60s, pacing beneath the awning of her residential hotel. She appears to be rehearsing dialogue with herself.

CORA

Ellen, I have no memory of this whatsoever. Ellen . . . Ellen I have NO memory of this whatsoever.

Jeff pulls the car up to the curb and Cora gets into the back seat.

5. INT. CAR. NIGHT. B/W.

NICOLE

Good morning, "Mom."

CORA

(gruff) Morning.

NICOLE

Sleep well?

CORA

Not a wink.

Cora immediately lights a cigarette. Nicole instinctively wrinkles her nose and turns away. Cora notices this and makes an exaggerated effort to keep the smoke away from Nicole by blowing it hard out the side of her mouth. Jeff glances back at the two women in the rearview mirror. No one speaks.

6. INT. SET. DAWN. B/W.

NICK—the Director, WOLF—the Cameraman and WANDA—the AD, stand in a loose triangle on the darkened set. All are holding coffee cups. The Gaffer can be seen in the background fumbling with a light.

NICK

Look, I'm not blaming anybody, Wanda. I'm just saying we left last night and I knew we didn't get that scene.

WANDA

I'm sorry, I thought it was a great scene, Nick.

NICK

It was OK; and it's going to be alright. But I'm not settling for OK today. This is a big scene and I'm not leaving till we get it.

WANDA

Whatever it takes, Nick. We're here for you.

NICK

Alright, here's what I'm thinking. Wolf, I want to do the whole scene in one shot.

WOLF

It's been done.

NICK

I know that but I'd like to try it anyway.

WOLF

Handheld.

NICK

No, dolly. We go from Close-up to Wide-shot and back to Close-up in the same shot.

WOLF

I'll use the 35, minimize distortion; I'll light it all from the ceiling. It could be kind of great.

WANDA

Sounds incredible. How long, Wolf?

WOLF

I'll need to see a couple run-throughs.

NICK

Not too many. It's a tough scene for the actors. I want them to feel relaxed, fresh . . .

WANDA

We've got all day, Nick. Whatever it takes. What do you think, Wolf—an hour, 45?

WOLF

I don't know how you drink that shit black, Nick. I got to dump in the milk. It's the only way I can cut the taste.

Suddenly the Gaffer turns on the 5K, flooding the room with harsh, blinding light.

NICK

Jesus!

WOLF

What the fuck?!

WANDA

Flame on, asshole!!

The screen goes completely WHITE.

7. **INT. SET APT. DAY. B/W.**

Screen is still white. Gradually it shifts back to proper exposure revealing NICOLE in Medium CU. Her eyes are riveting; it is obvious she is emotionally primed for the scene. A light meter is thrust in front of her face. She barely registers it.

WS, the entire Living Room set. Nicole sits on a sofa facing Cora seated opposite in an overstuffed chair. Two flats have been joined at right angles to create the Living Room corner. A table lamp and assorted framed photographs complete the rather scrawny looking set.

Most of the movie crew is seen, including Wolf looking through the camera.

WANDA

OK, picture's up. Quiet. Stop the work. Lock it up. Going for picture.

Nick approaches Nicole and Cora.

NICK

OK, nice and easy. Cora you're doing fine. Remember, really listen and really answer. (smiles at Nicole) I've got nothing to say to you. Just let it happen. It's all there.

WANDA

Ready, Nick?

WOLF

Look at this a second, Nick.

Nick moves behind the camera and looks through the eye-piece. Another CU of Nicole fills the frame. The image is visually and emotionally breathtaking.

WOLF

I pushed in a foot. She's incredible. It's coming right through the lens.

Nick grips Wolf's shoulder in gratitude.

NICK

That's great, man. Beautiful.

WANDA

Ready, Nick?

NICK

Let's go. Right away.

WANDA

And, roll sound.

SOUND

Speed!

WANDA

And, roll camera!

AC

Rolling!

CLAPPER

Scene six, take one. (hits the sticks)

NICK

Action.

8. INT. APT. THE "SCENE": TAKE 1. COLOR.

From the moment Nick calls "action" the film will cut directly to the shot the set camera is filming. The shot is fluid, graceful and in richly, beautiful COLOR. Nicole's performance is very strong; flawed only slightly by her nervousness.

NICOLE

Dad hit me first and knocked me down. It didn't hurt that much but I started crying anyway, hoping he would leave me alone. He went over and started hitting Danny.

CORA

Ellen, I have no memory of this whatsoever.

NICOLE

You were just standing there looking at me. Then you pulled me up and said, "You're not hurt." Like I was disgusting for faking, for doing the only thing I could think of to keep him from hitting me again.

CORA

I was worried about Danny.

NICOLE

You do remember.

Nick, the Director (Steve Buscemi), Wolf, the Cameraman (Dermot Mulroney), and the Assistant Cameraman (Kevin Corrigan) get ready for "action."
(Photo by Bill Bettencourt)

CORA

He was smaller than you.

Nicole turns to Cora with the heartbreaking gaze of an abandoned child. Nick and the rest of the crew watch in awe.

NICOLE

You were so worried about Danny—

Suddenly the BOOM dips all the way into the shot.

9. **INT. SET APT. DAY. B/W.**

WOLF

Cut! Boom in. Sorry, I had to cut. Les, your boom was all the way in the shot.

BOOM

Well, where's the frame line?

All the crew move around, all talking at once.

WANDA

OK, can we get a frame line? Hold it down. We're going again right away. Nobody moves. Les, you got the frame line?

BOOM

I guess so.

WANDA

OK, here we go. Right away. Picture's up.

Nick approaches Nicole and Cora.

NICK

Beautiful; both of you. Stay focused. Stay with it. No big deal. Let's go, Wanda. Right away.

WANDA

Roll sound!

SOUND

Speed!

WANDA

Roll camera!

AC

Rolling!

CLAPPER

Scene six, take two. (hits the sticks)

NICK

And, action.

10. INT. APT. THE "SCENE": TAKE 2. COLOR.

NICOLE

Dad hit me first and knocked me down. It didn't hurt that much but I started crying anyway, hoping he would leave me alone. He went over and started hitting Danny.

CORA

Ellen, I—

The image suddenly goes out of focus.

11. INT. SET APT. DAY. B/W.

AC

I'm sorry, I have to cut. I was completely off on the focus. It's my fault, I'm sorry.

WANDA

Thanks for the apology but you'll never work in this town again. (laughter)

AC

I've got it now.

WANDA

Here we go, right away. Lock it up. And roll sound . . .

SOUND

Speed!

WANDA

Roll Camera!

AC

Rolling!

CLAPPER

Scene six, take three. (hits the sticks)

> NICK

And, action.

12. INT. APT. THE "SCENE": TAKE 3. COLOR.

The scene begins once again. Remarkably, Nicole's enormous commitment is just as full and sharp. Nick is in ecstasy.

> NICOLE

Dad hit me first and knocked me down. It didn't hurt that much but I started crying anyway, hoping he would leave me alone. He went over and started hitting Danny.

> CORA

Ellen, I have no memory of this whatsoever.

Suddenly a car stops right outside, a heavy, bass-driven rap song blasting out of its trunk-mounted speakers.

13. INT. SET APT. DAY. B/W.

> SOUND

Street noise!

> WANDA

That's a cut! (into her walkie) What the fuck's going on down there!? You call that a lock-up!? Get that car out of there!

> NICK

Jesus Christ. Why doesn't the guy just get a flat-

bed trailer with about 600 speakers on it and tow
it behind his car.

Everyone nods in annoyed agreement; everyone except the
Boom man who appears to be following the music with the
mike, bopping to it through the headphones. Slowly, inter-
minably, the music fades off into the distance.

SOUND

And . . . it's clear.

WANDA

(into her walkie) Do I have a lock-up?

WALKIE (vo)

kkkkkssst . . . sttttss yes.

WANDA

Is that a real lock-up?

WALKIE (vo)

sssssssssssssppppkkss.

WANDA

OK, right away. Picture's up. Roll sound.

SOUND

Speed!

WANDA

And, roll camera!

AC

Rolling!

CLAPPER

Scene six, take four. (hits the sticks)

NICK

Action.

14. INT. SET APT. THE "SCENE": TAKE 4. COLOR.

NICOLE

Dad hit me first and knocked me down. It didn't hurt that much but I started crying anyway, hoping he would leave me alone. He went over and started hitting Danny.

CORA

Ellen, I have no memory of this whatsoever.

NICOLE

You were just standing there looking at me. Then you pulled—

Suddenly the BOOM drops into frame again.

15. INT. SET APT. DAY. B/W.

WOLF

Boom's in.

NICK

Jesus Christ.

BOOM

Where?

WOLF

The whole left side of frame, Les.

WANDA

Alright, can we please get a motherfucking frame line please?!

BOOM

The frame keeps changing.

WOLF

That's the idea, Les.

SOUND

May I make a suggestion? Is it possible to maybe break the shot down? Maybe two shots instead? Might make it easier for Les.

NICK

No.

SOUND

Then I need ten minutes to switch to radio mikes.

WANDA

Your call, Nick.

NICK

There won't be any other sound problems?

SOUND

No more boom problems.

NICK

Switch to radios.

WANDA

That's a ten-minute break. Release the lock-up. Stand by.

WOLF

(to the AC) Get me a coffee. Half milk.

16. INT. SET APT. DAY. B/W.

Nick looks for Nicole but sees only Cora standing by the couch. Les has both arms up the back of her dress, running the wire to her radio mike. She's wearing stockings rolled down to just above her knees.

Nick turns and spots Nicole by herself in a dark corner of the set and walks over to her.

17. INT. SET APT. A CORNER. DAY. B/W.

NICK

I'm sorry about all this, Nicole.

NICOLE

It's not your fault, Nick. Is there a way to use some of the earlier takes?

NICK

Not unless I change the shot; do a cutaway of Cora or something and intercut the takes. I don't want to do that. It's a really nice shot and what you're doing is incredible.

NICOLE

Thanks, Nick.

NICK

The radio mikes are going to make everything easier. So, look. Take a moment. Let all this shit go. We don't roll till you're ready.

NICOLE

OK.

Nick moves back to the set, leaving Nicole in the shadows. Camera stays on her as she begins emotionally preparing herself once again.

PAM (vo)

How was she in that Richard Gere movie?

CYBIL (vo)

So-so.

Camera slips halfway through an open bedroom door, holding Nicole on one side of the frame while revealing PAM the Script Supervisor and CYBIL sitting on the floor smoking. Though separated by the wall, Nicole hears everything the two women say.

PAM

Her career really took off, didn't it?

CYBIL

I saw her in a Michael Bolton video.

PAM

She is nice; but I could do a better job.

Camera slips into a CU of Nicole. She closes her eyes as the two women continue talking about her. Screen goes BLACK.

18. INT. SET APT. DAY. B/W.

A BLACK scrim, held by the Gaffer, passes in front of the camera, revealing the set with Nicole and Cora settling in for a take.

WANDA

Where's that flag going?

GAFFER

It's a scrim.

WANDA

Wolf!

WOLF

Two seconds, Wanda.

WANDA

No. No more tweaking. Picture's up. (into her walkie) Lock it up!

Wolf quickly motions Gaffer to hand-hold the scrim in front of the 5K.

WANDA

And, roll sound.

SOUND

Speed!

WANDA

Roll camera!

AC

Rolling!

CLAPPER

Scene six, take five. (hits the sticks)

NICK

Action.

19. INT. SET APT. THE "SCENE": TAKE 5. COLOR.

Once again the scene begins. Nicole shows the first signs of losing her concentration.

NICOLE

Dad hit me first and knocked me down. It didn't hurt that much but I started crying anyway, hoping he would leave me alone. He went over and started hitting Danny.

CORA

Ellen, I have no memory—

Suddenly there is a tremendous EXPLOSION sending bits of glass flying through the frame. Cora jumps, clutching her chest.

CORA

Oh, God!

20. INT. SET APT. DAY. B/W.

CU the light the Gaffer had been holding the scrim before.
It is smoking and shattered.

NICK

Jesus fucking Christ!

WOLF

(to the Gaffer) Kill it. Kill it. Pull the plug. Right
there by your foot.

WANDA

That's a cut. Anybody hurt? Cora, are you alright?

Cora nods wordlessly, gasping for breath.

WANDA

Props. Props! Let's get a broom up here right
away. Clear the set!

21. INT. APT. HALLWAY. DAY. B/W.

Nick, Cora, and Nicole stand in a corner of the landing.
Nick is making obvious attempts to lighten the mood.

NICK

Well, let's see. What do you think is going to happen next, Cora?

CORA

I'm going to have a heart attack!

NICK

No, you're not. You're going in there in two min-

utes and we are really going to nail this scene. I
know it. I have no doubt about it. Nicole . . .

Nick turns to Nicole and stops in midsentence. He looks at
her for a long moment. Nicole returns his gaze then suddenly looks away.

                    WANDA (vo)

Nick! Nick!

                      NICK

One second!

Nick hesitates a moment then rushes back to the set.

                      CORA

I'll tell you this much right now; I am never, ever
doing another fucking low-budget movie.

22. INT. SET APT. DAY. B/W.

Nick joins Wanda and Wolf on the set couch and chair.

                      NICK

What's up?

                     WANDA

Wolf and I were talking . . . Ellen's losing it a little
bit. You got three quarters of the scene really,
really incredible in the first take. Do a quick cutaway and all you need is a pickup of the last part
of the scene.

                      NICK

Wolf?

WOLF

You know how I feel; I love this shot. Hell, I designed it.

NICK

Then let's just stick with the game plan, OK? It's a simple shot. We're going to get it this time, I feel it.

WANDA

We're here for you, Nick. Whatever it takes.

Nick moves off. Wanda stares at Wolf who studiously inspects his light meter.

WANDA

Thanks.

23. **INT. SET APT. DAY. B/W.**

Camera is close on the black-and-white clapboard. Nicole's face can be partially seen behind it.

WANDA

And, roll sound.

SOUND

Speed!

WANDA

And, roll camera!

AC

Rolling!

Nicole (Catherine Keener) steels herself for another take.
(Photo by Bill Bettencourt)

CLAPPER

Scene six, take six. (hits the sticks)

NICK

Action.

24. INT. SET APT. THE "SCENE": TAKE 6. COLOR.

As the scene begins again, it is obvious that both actresses are completely distracted. Nick's face betrays a rapidly increasing anxiety.

NICOLE

Dad hit me first and knocked me down. It didn't hurt that much but I started crying anyway, hoping he would leave me alone. He went over and started hitting Danny.

CORA

I . . .

There is a long awkward pause as Cora realizes she can't remember her line.

25. INT. SET APT. DAY. B/W.

NICK

Cut. That's OK, Cora. What's the line? Just say it to me; no acting.

CORA

I . . . (pause)

AC

"Ellen, I have no memory of this line whatsoever."

Amid general tittering from the crew, Wanda yells out.

WANDA

OK, could we get the line please?! Script!

SCRIPT (Pam)

"Ellen, I have no memory of this whatsoever."

WANDA

Thank you. And, roll sound.

SOUND

Speed!

WANDA

And, roll camera!

AC

Rolling!

CLAPPER

Scene six, take seven. (hits the sticks)

NICK

Action.

26. **INT. SET APT. THE "SCENE": TAKE 7. COLOR.**

The scene begins again. Nicole is lifeless; she's merely saying the lines.

NICOLE

Dad hit me first and knocked me down. It didn't hurt that much but I started crying anyway—

> CORA

I was worried about Danny!

Nicole stops cold, completely thrown by Cora jumping her line.

> NICOLE

I'm sorry, I'm lost . . .

27. INT. SET APT. DAY. B/W.

> NICK

Cut. It's OK. No big deal.

Nick's voice has the rigid tremble of someone barely able to keep from screaming.

> NICK

Everyone relax. We're just going to run the lines. That's all. No acting. Just run the lines. Then we're going to shoot this fucking scene.

28. INT. SET APT. THE COUCH. DAY. B/W.

Nicole gets up quietly and sits next to Cora on the couch, wordlessly taking her hand in hers.

> CORA

(whispers) I'm so sorry. I'm fucking this up for you.

> NICOLE

(whispers) Cora, don't even think that. You're doing great. I'm the one who's fucking it up. If I get through this I swear I'm never acting again.

She means it. Cora glances up at her, seeing for the first time how pain and defeat have drawn the life from Nicole's face. On an impulse Cora reaches out and gently lifts a strand of Nicole's hair from her eyes.

A sudden amazed alarm fills Nicole. The living room grows strangely quiet.

NICK

(faintly, from a distance) And, action on the run-through.

CU Nicole. She looks quickly toward Nick in confusion.

29. INT. HOSPITAL ROOM. DAY. COLOR.

DISSOLVE to a nurse moving quickly past the camera and out the open door of the hospital room.

CU Nicole, seated on the edge of the hospital bed. Still confused, she looks down at the old woman lying in the bed. The woman's face is pale and drawn. As Nicole leans closer her mother reaches out and gently brushes a strand of hair away from her face. The gesture is one of love, acceptance, and farewell. It is identical to the one we have just seen Cora make to her.

NICK (vo)

And action on the run-through.

30. INT. SET APT. DAY. B/W.

WS, the Living Room Set. Nick, Wanda, the rest of the crew standing quietly. Nicole glances over at Cora and instantly something unspoken and unexplained passes between them. The run-through begins.

From the moment Nicole opens her mouth it is obvious there has been a remarkable change in her. Every word now has the stunning clarity of truth. Cora is completely engulfed in the moment.

NICOLE

Dad hit me first and knocked me down. It didn't hurt that much but I started crying anyway, hoping he would leave me alone. He went over and started hitting Danny.

CORA

Ellen, I have no memory of this whatsoever.

NICOLE

You were just standing there looking at me.

As Nicole continues, one by one the crew turn and watch this exquisite moment happening before them. Nick's face is lit with rapture.

NICK

(whispering) Roll camera . . . roll camera.

He glances over and to his horror sees that no one is behind the camera. He whispers frantically to the AC.

NICK

Where's Wolf?

AC

(whispers) In the bathroom . . . he doesn't feel good.

> NICK

(whispers) Get him! Get him!

Nick turns back to the scene, watching its beauty now in
agony.

> NICOLE

Then you pulled me up and said, "You're not
hurt." Like I was disgusting for faking, for doing
the only thing I could think of to keep him from
hitting me again.

> CORA

I was worried about Danny.

> NICOLE

You do remember.

> CORA

He was smaller than you.

> NICOLE

You were so worried about Danny. What about
me, Mom? Why weren't you worried about me?

There is a heavy, stunned silence as the scene ends. Nicole
and Cora are in each other's arms. Pam and Cybil share a
piece of tissue. CUT TO: an extreme CU of Nick.

> NICK

Where the fuck is Wolf?!!!

31. INT. BATHROOM. DAY. B/W.

In the cramped confines of the dingy basement bathroom,
Wolf pukes violently into the toilet. His face is pale and

slick with perspiration. His eyes look upward toward the sound of Nick yelling.

WOLF

One second!

Wolf tries to continue but another spasm of nausea wrenches him back toward the toilet bowl.

32. INT. SET APT. THE COUCH. DAY. B/W.

The set is quiet, subdued. Nick sits on the couch with Nicole and Cora. Wolf sits groggily behind the camera wiping the sweat from his face. Wanda addresses the crew.

WANDA

OK, listen up. Nobody drinks the milk downstairs. OK? It appears to be bad.

Nick speaks uneasily to Nicole and Cora. He is a wreck and his insistent smile of encouragement looks absolutely demented.

NICK

I've had to, well I've changed the shot; we're just a little pressed for time. It'll just be a CU of Ellen for the last part of the scene, starting with Cora's "I was worried about Danny." OK? I'll find a way to cut this into the fourth take. We almost had it. That was unbelievable, both of you. But let's not think about it. That moment is gone, and . . . we'll, we'll get another one. I have no doubt about it. OK? Here we go.

Nick walks over and stands beside the camera.

33. INT. SET APT. BY THE CAMERA. DAY. B/W.

WOLF

I'm ready, Nick.

Nick is so angry he can't even look at Wolf.

                    NICK

Call it, Wanda.

                    WANDA

And, roll sound.

                    SOUND

Speed!

                    WANDA

And, roll camera!

                    AC

Rolling!

                    CLAPPER

Scene six, Pickup, take one. (hits the sticks)

                    NICK

Action.

34. INT. SET APT. THE "SCENE": PICKUP 1. COLOR.

The scene begins at the pickup point. Miraculously, both Cora and Nicole are just as concentrated and engaged as they were in the run-through.

                    CORA

I was worried about Danny.

                    NICOLE

You do remember.

CORA

He was smaller than you.

NICOLE

You were so worried about Danny. What about me, Mom? Why weren't—

In the middle of this final, delicate moment an insistent electronic beeping is heard.

35. INT. SET APT. DAY. B/W.

NICK

CUT!!!!

WANDA

What the fuck is that?! Sound?

SOUND

(frantically checking his equipment) It's not me.

BOOM

It's the camera.

WOLF

The fuck it is. It's off; it's not even running.

The beep continues, growing louder.

WANDA

(into her walkie) What's going on down there?! Do I have a lock-up?! Nothing? You don't hear a beep-ing sound? (to Nick) The street's quiet.

NICK

Then what the fuck is it!!?

AC

It's somebody's watch!

Everybody holds their watches up to their ears.

WOLF

Not mine.

WANDA

Not mine.

SOUND

Not mine.

BOOM

Not mine.

And so on, until all watches have been checked with negative results. The beeping continues, growing louder and louder.

Suddenly Nick loses it. He starts running around the set, ripping things apart, knocking over tables, lamps, chairs. He shoves Cora off the couch and whips off the cushions, heaving them against the wall with a startling violence.

NICK

Where is it!! You motherfucker! You cock-sucking motherfucking bastard! Where the fuck are you!? Where!! Where!!

Everyone watches Nick demolish the set in stunned, open-mouthed amazement. Nick turns to the crew in rage.

NICK

Can someone help me please?! Do I have to do everything myself here?!

Nick loses it completely.

NICK

Hey, Cora. Why don't you go learn your lines! Hey Scriptgirl, are you finally going to pay attention here?! Hey, focus puller, you want to make a movie or get stoned?! Huh, I got some great fuckin' Thai Stick here! Hey Wolf, you pretentious, beret-wearing motherfucker! I saw your reel, man; it sucked! Who the hell would hire you anyway! Hey Wanda, next time can you wear a shirt that's a little more distracting to my actors! (to the Gaffer) Hey Bob! Hi Bob! Can you please make a little more noise on the dolly you creaky motherfucker! (to Cybil) What is your name!? What do you fucking do around here?! (to the Soundman) Hey Speedo, what's the matter? Can't even find a teeny fucking beep?!

CU of Nicole. She turns away, unable to watch anymore. The beeping continues.

NICK

See what I have to put up with, Nicole!? Maybe next time you'll do some of that magic on camera!? But no, no—wait till Wolf is puking his guts out, "Oh now I'll be good!!"

WS, the entire room. Nick's last word echoes throughout the silent set. Suddenly he stops in the center of the demolished set and lets out a long, wrenching scream.

36. INT. BEDROOM. NIGHT. COLOR.

QUICK CUT TO extreme CU Nick's face, just as his eyes open. The film is in COLOR now. The room is in heavy darkness except for the light on Nick's face. Nick reaches over and shuts off his clock radio. The digital dial shows 4:00 A.M. The beeping finally stops.

Nick turns on a light and sits up in bed, drenched in sweat and still breathing heavily.

NICK

God . . . (this is not a sigh of relief)

The camera DOLLIES swiftly back away from Nick. He stares at it in stunned amazement. Just then a DOOR closes right into the lens turning the frame into complete BLACKNESS.

Two

Out of the BLACKNESS a door opens away from the camera revealing WANDA looking into her closet (the camera is inside the closet). From this point on, the rest of the film is in COLOR except where specifically indicated to be Black and White.

37. INT. WANDA'S APT. DAWN.

She is wearing only a bra, black stretch pants, and cowboy boots. She rummages quickly through some blouses, selects the same garish one she wore in Part One, then walks away revealing WOLF sitting on the edge of the rumpled bed. He is dressed exactly the same as when we last saw him, complete with beret. He struggles groggily into his socks and boots. The entire apartment is in disarray. A bedside clock reads 4:13 A.M.

WOLF

Well, when did he ask you?

WANDA

Yesterday, when I was helping him check into his hotel.

WOLF

What, the guy can't even check into a hotel by himself?

WANDA

Listen, Wolf, having Chad Palomino in this movie will benefit us all. If being there when he checks

into his hotel makes him feel better, then I'm
happy to do it.

WOLF

Well, how did it come up?

WANDA

He asked me if I liked jazz, I said yes, and he suggested we meet tonight at a jazz club.

WOLF

I like jazz.

WANDA

He did not invite you. (applies perfume)

WOLF

Why are you wearing perfume to work?

WANDA

Because I feel like it.

WOLF

You didn't wear it yesterday.

WANDA

Oh, stop it. You're acting like a child.

Wanda playfully swipes at Wolf's face with a negligee she
is returning to the closet. It misses him completely.

WOLF

My eye!

WANDA

Oh, God. Sweetheart, are you alright?

WOLF

Do I look alright?!

WANDA

Let me see. Christ, we're going to be late.

Wanda sits and perfunctorily examines Wolf's eye.

38. INT. CAR. DAWN.

The car is parked outside a rather seedy hotel. JEFF, the Intern and NICK, the Director, sit quietly in the motionless car.

NICK

Should we call up to the room again?

JEFF

He said he'd be right down.

Nick lets out a huge yawn.

JEFF

Tired?

NICK

I'm exhausted. I dreamt I was on the set all night. I was just trying to do one shot and everything kept going wrong.

JEFF

That's an anxiety dream. Are you anxious about something?

NICK

I don't know. Sometimes I wonder what the hell I'm doing in this business. It's all just one compromise and disappointment after another. I don't know if I have the personality for it.

JEFF

Sounds kind of like an identity crisis.

NICK

Maybe you're right. Who am I? What am I really capable of? Maybe I should just get a job teaching at a women's college somewhere.

JEFF

How'd you get into cinematography?

NICK

I'm not a cinematographer.

JEFF

You're not?

NICK

No. I'm directing this movie.

JEFF

(pause) How'd you get into directing?

39. INT. HOTEL ROOM. DAWN.

In the dim light of the hotel room, CHAD PALOMINO dresses quickly. He is young, handsome, with long blond hair. A WOMAN sits nude on the bed, her back to the camera. The faint sound of a shower comes from the adjacent bathroom.

PALOMINO

They're waiting downstairs.

WOMAN

Go ahead, I'll take a taxi.

PALOMINO

Oh, OK. Listen, I've got to tell you, I had a lot of fun last night, really, but for me, where I'm at right now in my life, a relationship is . . .

WOMAN

Chad; hold it. This was a one-time deal. You know it, I know it. There is no need for melodrama.

PALOMINO

I just thought you might . . .

WOMAN

Look, all I ask is that you don't mention this to anyone.

PALOMINO

Hey, that's not my style.

WOMAN

Good.

PALOMINO

So, I'll see you on the set.

Palomino slips out the door. The woman falls back onto the bed, turning her face toward the camera. We see it is NICOLE.

NICOLE

God damn it.

She lies for a moment, listening to the sound of the shower. The bedside clock reads 4:30 A.M.

40. **INT. CAR. DAWN.**

The car pulls up outside a NYC apt building. Jeff, Nick, and Palomino sit inside.

PALOMINO

I got two films coming up right after yours, Nick. One I play a rapist that Michelle Pfeiffer falls in love with. The other I'm kind of a sexy serial killer who shacks up with Winona Ryder.

NICK

That's great, man.

PALOMINO

Yeah, but I'm not into that hostess twinkie shit, Nick.

NICK

Hostess twinkie?

PALOMINO

That Hollywood shit. It's all fluff, man. These are the kind of movies I want to do, right here.

NICK

I'm glad you feel that way, Chad. And I just want to tell you, I'm really happy we can work together.

PALOMINO

Hey, me too! You're a great director, man. Your films are wacked! And I'm gonna be watching you, buddy. Like a hawk. I want to learn from you, Nick. I'm gonna pick your brain.

NICK

Good. Then you can pick my nose.

PALOMINO

(big laugh) See what I mean? You're wacked. Hey, what are we sitting here for?

NICK

We're waiting for Nicole.

PALOMINO

Nicole? She's takin' a tax—(he stops)

NICK

What?

PALOMINO

Probably taking a shower or something. Hey, how was her shower scene in that Richard Gere movie?

NICK

Good.

JEFF

Really great.

The three men sit in silence. WS, showing the car parked outside Nicole's apt, the men inside waiting.

41. INT. THE SET. MORNING.

A small, elegant bedroom set has been constructed in the middle of the huge empty space. One wall has a fake window. The GAFFER lies on the bed staring absently at the AC sitting motionless beside the camera a few feet away. Neither speaks for a long moment.

GAFFER

I think we got nudity today.

AC

(reads from his callsheet) It just says "Scene Six: Ellen and Damian kiss."

GAFFER

Could be a kiss with nudity.

AC

I like Ellen. She's my type.

GAFFER

Why is that?

AC

She's pretty. Smart. Kind of kooky.

Tom DiCillo discusses a scene with Catherine Keener.
(Photo by Bill Bettencourt)

GAFFER

Maybe I'll give her a part. That's right; I'm makin'
my own movie pretty soon.

AC

Oh yeah?

GAFFER

Yup. Feature. I brought my script.

The Gaffer tugs a thin, tattered SCRIPT, folded length-
wise, out of his back pocket.

GAFFER

Palomino's perfect for the lead. I'm going to give it
to him right during lunch. Maybe right after.

AC

Alright.

GAFFER

Got to be aggressive. You want to shoot it?

AC

Sure.

GAFFER

You ever shot anything?

AC

No.

GAFFER

That's alright; got to start somewhere.

Suddenly the Gaffer reaches out and warmly shakes the AC's hand.

42. INT. MAKEUP CORNER. DAY.

Nicole sits before the makeup mirror. LORDE, the male Makeup artist picks up a tube of Preparation H and begins applying it under Nicole's eyes just as Nick walks up.

NICK

Jesus, what are you doing?

LORDE

Shrinking tissue. That's what this stuff is for. Let that sit for two minutes, pumpkin; I'll be right back.

NICK

How'd you get here?

NICOLE

Took a taxi.

NICK

Oh. We've been waiting in front of your apartment for half an hour.

NICOLE

God, I'm sorry, Nick. Something came up. I forgot to call. I'm sorry, I feel like such an asshole.

NICK

You're just saying that because you have Preparation H on your face.

NICOLE

I never should have gone out last night. I hate jazz. God, I look terrible.

NICK

No you don't.

NICOLE

Don't bullshit me, Nick.

NICK

I'm not. You really look beautiful.

Something in Nick's voice makes Nicole glance up at him. He looks away quickly. The moment is awkward, as if they both realize he has inadvertently revealed something. Just then Palomino approaches.

PALOMINO

Hey! How'd you get here, Nicole?

NICOLE

I took a cab.

PALOMINO

Oh, cause we were wondering how you got here.

Nick looks at both of them in a moment of silence.

NICK

Alright, good; everybody's here. We'll do a run-through as soon as you guys are ready.

PALOMINO

You got it, Chief.

Lorde reenters as Nick leaves. Palomino sits in the chair beside Nicole and Lorde immediately begins his makeup. No one speaks.

43. INT. THE SET. DAY.

The crew is assembled behind the camera. Wolf is now wearing a black eyepatch over one eye. Nick is on the set, talking with Nicole and Palomino. Palomino wears a tuxedo and Nicole is in an elaborate low-cut gown.

WANDA

Hold it down, hold it down, people. Actors working.

PALOMINO

Great shirt, Wanda.

WANDA

(big smile) Why, thank you, Chad.

NICK

OK, let's work out the rest of this blocking. Wolf— (notices Wolf's eyepatch) What happened to your eye?

WOLF

A little accident.

NICK

You going to be alright?

WOLF

I think so.

PALOMINO

It looks good on you, man.

NICK

Nicole is standing here, Chad, you're there by the chair. Camera is close on Ellen: her first line.

ELLEN

I've always admired you from afar.

DAMIAN

Admired? That sounds rather professional.

NICK

Good! "Professional," that's the cue; Damian steps up to the bed. Camera pulls back. The scene continues.

ELLEN

Well, then: loved. How does that sound?

DAMIAN

It sounds like the champagne talking.

ELLEN

I've loved you from the moment we met.

DAMIAN

Why didn't you tell me?

ELLEN

We were working together. I didn't want anything to interfere.

DAMIAN

God. And all this time I thought . . .

NICK

Then the kiss. How's that feel?

PALOMINO

Great.

NICK

Nicole?

NICOLE

Good.

NICK

Wolf, any thoughts?

WOLF

Nope.

PALOMINO

I've got a thought. What about Damian having an eyepatch like Wolf's?

NICK

Let me think about that one, Chad.

PALOMINO

OK, you're the genius. Nick Reve, Living in Oblivion, Scene Six, Take One. Let's shoot it!

NICK

One second, Chad. You ready for one, Wolf?

WOLF

Hell, I been ready.

PALOMINO

Alright, Wolfman.

NICK

Good. Call it, Wanda.

WANDA

Going for picture. Lock it up. And roll sound.

SOUND

Speed!

WANDA

Roll camera!

AC

Rolling!

CLAPPER

Scene six, take one!

NICK

And, action.

44. INT. THE SET. TAKE ONE.

Instantly the film cuts from color to B/W. Chad and Nicole begin their Love Scene.

ELLEN

I've always admired you from afar.

DAMIAN

Admired? That sounds rather professional.

The camera starts to dolly, however Chad does not move. He goes out of frame forcing Wolf to pan abruptly to Nicole.

ELLEN

Well, then: loved. How does that sound?

DAMIAN

It sounds like the champagne talking.

ELLEN

I've loved you from the moment we met.

DAMIAN

(finally moves to his mark) Why didn't you tell me?

ELLEN

We were working together. I didn't want anything to interfere.

DAMIAN

God. And all this time I thought . . .

Palomino and Nicole embrace. Their kiss, like the entire scene, is flat, lifeless, and awful.

45. INT. THE SET.

NICK

Cut. Very good.

WOLF

Not for camera. Chad was completely out of frame.

NICK

Yeah, Chad; what happened, buddy? Forget your cue?

PALOMINO

Oh no, man. I held back. It really felt like something Damian would do; holding back to the last moment.

NICK

Oh, I see. How's that for you, Wolf?

WOLF

I don't care when he moves. Just give me a fucking cue.

PALOMINO

The Lone Wolf!

NICK

What line did he move on?

SCRIPT

"Why didn't you tell me?"

NICK

Alright, "me" is the new cue. Nicole, how does that feel to you?

NICOLE

Fine, if that's what Chad wants to do.

PALOMINO

"Me, me, me," that's the cue. Let's shoot; I'm stoked!

NICK

One second, Chad.

Nick approaches the bed and speaks quietly to Chad and Nicole.

NICK

Chad, how would you describe this scene, in one word?

PALOMINO

Great. It's a great scene, man.

NICK

No, I mean it's a love scene. Right?

PALOMINO

Definitely.

NICK

These two people really love each other. And we
want to see that, especially in the kiss.

PALOMINO

Hey, say no more, Chief.

NICK

Nicole?

NICOLE

I understand, Chief.

NICK

Good. Here we go. Call it, Wanda.

WANDA

Going for picture. Lock it up. And roll sound.

SOUND

Speed!

WANDA

Roll camera!

AC

Rolling!

CLAPPER

Scene six, take two!

NICK

And, action.

46. INT. THE SCENE. TAKE TWO. DAY.

ELLEN

I've always admired you from afar.

Palomino moves immediately to the bed, changing his blocking and causing the camera crew and Nicole considerable confusion.

DAMIAN

Admired? That sounds rather professional.

ELLEN

Well, then: loved. How does that sound?

DAMIAN

It sounds like the champagne talking.

ELLEN

I've loved you from the moment we met.

DAMIAN

Why didn't you tell me?

ELLEN

We were working together. I didn't want anything to interfere.

DAMIAN

God. And all this time I thought . . .

The scene once again is awful. Nick gives their listless kiss a few moments then calls CUT.

47. INT. THE SET. DAY.

NICK

And, cut. Very good. Wolf?

WOLF

Chad missed his cue again; the whole dolly is unusable.

NICK

Yeah, Chad. What happened; I thought you were going to hold back till "me"?

PALOMINO

The more I thought about it the more it didn't seem right. And I'm thinking, watch me here, instead of coming around the bed, what if I just slip here like this and do the whole scene lying down?

NICK

I don't know, that seems a little . . .

PALOMINO

Hey, I'm just throwing out ideas here. Trying to get the juices flowing.

NICK

Nicole, how does that feel to you?

NICOLE

Well, I can turn to look at him. But won't you be shooting the back of my head?

Tom DiCillo (center) sets up a shot with cinematographer Frank Prinzi (right). Kevin Corrigan (left) playing the Assistant Cameraman, looks on intently, picking their brains.
(Photo by Bill Bettencourt)

WOLF

Plus Chad is completely out of the light down there.

PALOMINO

Hey, Wolf; I'm not worried about my face, man. It's about the acting; that's all I care about.

WOLF

It's your call, Nick. His acting or his face.

NICK

For some reason I was hoping we could get both. (laughs) I thought that's what we were trying to do here.

WOLF

I'll have to set another light.

WANDA

We're ahead of schedule, Nick. I think we can afford a few minutes to set a light for Mr. Palomino.

NICK

Good, let's do it. Ellen, Damian; let's talk for a second.

As Nick, Nicole, and Palomino step off the set Wanda speaks to the crew in general.

WANDA

We'll pause to set this light and go again right away. How long, Wolf?

Wolf doesn't answer, though he stands a mere foot away, watching the Gaffer set up a light.

WANDA

Wolf?

Wolf walks away from Wanda without a word. The entire crew watches this.

48. INT. A CORNER. DAY.

Nick, Palomino, and Nicole confer, all three smoking.

NICK

OK, let's make sure we know what's going on here. These two people have loved each other for years, each of them not knowing the other was in love with them. And tonight, in this little room it all comes out. It's like a dam bursting. Does that make sense? Nicole?

NICOLE

It makes perfect sense. I just haven't found it yet. I'll get it though.

NICK

What about you, Chad?

PALOMINO

I'm there, man. I got the dam going, the river, everything. You watch, that little change in the blocking is going to open the whole scene up for me.

WANDA (vo)

We're ready, Nick!

NICK

Good. Let's go.

49. INT. THE SET. DAY.

WANDA

Going for picture. Lock it up. And roll sound.

SOUND

Speed!

WANDA

Roll camera!

AC

Rolling!

CLAPPER

Scene six, take three!

NICK

And, action.

50. INT. THE SCENE. TAKE THREE. DAY.

ELLEN

I've always admired you from afar.

Palomino saunters over and sprawls on the bed, forcing Nicole to turn her head completely away from the camera.

DAMIAN

Admired? That sounds rather professional.

ELLEN

Well, then: loved. How does that sound?

DAMIAN

It sounds like the champagne talking.

ELLEN

I've loved you from the moment we met.

DAMIAN

Why didn't you tell me?

ELLEN

We were working together—I'm sorry, can we cut, Nick?

51. INT. THE SET. DAY.

NICK

Cut!

WANDA

That's a cut!

PALOMINO

Dammit! That was a good one!

NICOLE

I know, I'm sorry. But this feels really awkward; turning all the way around like this.

NICK

Yeah, I think the lying on the bed is not quite

working, Chad. Let's try one with the original
blocking.

PALOMINO

Which one was that? There's been so many damn
changes. Could somebody help me out please?

SCRIPT

The cue for the original blocking is "professional."

PALOMINO

(intimate) Thank you. Thank you very much.

NICK

OK, right away. Call it, Wanda.

NICOLE

Nick? Could I just have a moment? Is that alright?

NICK

Of course, Nicole; are you kidding? Hold the roll,
Wanda.

WANDA

Holding the roll!

Nicole remains seated on the bed, lowering her head and
closing her eyes as she attempts to generate some emotion
for the scene. Everyone watches her in complete silence.

52. **INT. NEAR THE CAMERA. DAY.**

Palomino tiptoes over to the camera where Wanda and the
Scriptgirl are standing side by side. As he leans between

them, checking his lines on the Scriptgirl's script, he inhales deeply then exhales with a barely audible sigh.

PALOMINO

(whispers) Someone over here smells very, very nice.

Thinking he means her, Wanda's lips flutter in a brief, involuntary smile. Meanwhile, the Scriptgirl turns away, blushing furiously.

53. INT. THE SET. DAY.

Palomino tiptoes again back to his spot. Nicole raises her head and nods once to Nick. She seems to have aroused some real emotion in herself.

NICK

(with quiet intensity) Call it, Wanda.

WANDA

And roll sound.

SOUND

Speed!

WANDA

Roll camera!

AC

Rolling!

CLAPPER

Scene six, take four!

PALOMINO

(suddenly) Nick, I just had a great idea!

WANDA

Hold the roll!

NICK

What is it, Chad?

PALOMINO

Just stop me if I'm out of line here, but she says "admired from afar," right? Doesn't it make sense to see Damian up close and her "afar?" You start on a Close-up of Damian, watch me here; as she declares her love, the camera moves with me into this primo two-shot that you and the Wolfmeister have set up here.

NICK

What do you think, Wolf?

WOLF

I don't like it. This is Ellen's scene.

NICK

I don't know; it sort of makes sense.

PALOMINO

Hey, you did it, man. It's all there in the writing.

WOLF

I'd have to relight.

Nick pauses, thinking hard.

WANDA

We're still ahead of schedule, Nick; if that means anything to you.

NICK

Let's do it.

WOLF

(to the Gaffer) Get me a tweenie right here, with diffusion.

WANDA

OK, everyone stand by. We're pausing briefly to set one little light, then we're going again, right away. Stand-in please for Mr. Palomino.

GAFFER

I'll do it.

WOLF

Get the fucking light!

54. INT. CRAFT SERVICE TABLE. DAY.

Several members of the crew loiter around the table. The Scriptgirl approaches carrying a donut in one hand and a cup of coffee in the other. Palomino notices her and moves quietly to her side. Without a word he picks up the milk and pours some in her coffee. Nicole stands nearby and watches the following exchange.

SCRIPT

Thanks.

PALOMINO

My pleasure. Sugar?

SCRIPT

Just a bit.

Palomino puts sugar in her coffee with extreme care.

PALOMINO

You like jazz?

SCRIPT

Very much.

PALOMINO

Maybe we could go hear some tonight.

Palomino smiles and moves away just as Wanda comes up for a coffee refill.

WANDA

It's going well I think. Don't you think?

SCRIPT

Very well. What time do you think we'll finish?

WANDA

Early I hope. I'm going to a jazz club tonight.

SCRIPT

Really? So am I. He's wonderful, isn't he?

WANDA

Chad?

SCRIPT

He's so natural, like . . . air.

Nicole approaches.

SCRIPT

I wonder what his sign is. Do you know, Nicole?

NICOLE

I don't know his sign, but I think his moon is in
Uranus.

Wanda chokes hard on her coffee as Nicole walks off with
a bitter smile.

SCRIPT

You don't have to be nasty.

55. INT. THE SET. DAY.

Palomino saunters onto the set as Wolf and his crew finish
relighting.

PALOMINO

Yo, Wolfman. Is this my new mark?

WOLF

Until you change it. Where's my fucking eyepatch?!

Wolf walks off. The Gaffer slips the AC a shrewd wink then
walks over and stands next to Palomino, giving him a big,
friendly grin.

GAFFER

Hey, Chad.

PALOMINO

Hey, whatya say.

GAFFER

I'm Bob. I'm lighting this show.

PALOMINO

Chad Palomino; Actor.

GAFFER

(big smile) I know.

PALOMINO

(to the ac) Hey, what's your name?

AC

Maurice.

PALOMINO

Maurice! Hey, Maurice Chevalier! Any relation?
Probably not. Hey, smoking crew guys, really.

The Gaffer slips his own script out of his back pocket and
begins leafing through it.

GAFFER

Hey thanks, Chad. Actually I wrote a script.

PALOMINO

Oh, yeah?

Palomino takes the Gaffer's script and holds it up to his eyes, shading them from a light he's looking at across the room. He points to the light.

PALOMINO

Hey, Bill. See that light over there?

GAFFER

Uh, yeah.

PALOMINO

Lower it about three feet.

Palomino hands the Gaffer back his script and walks off. The Gaffer and AC stand in silence for a long awkward moment.

56. INT. BATHROOM. DAY.

Nick intently scrutinizes himself in the mirror. Leaning closer he makes a careful adjustment to the way his hair falls over his ear, then steps back to examine himself.

NICK

Would you care to have a drink tonight? Hey, Nicole, what do you say you and I have a drink tonight?

Suddenly the door opens behind him and Nicole walks in.

NICOLE

Oh, Nick! I'm sorry!

NICK

That's OK, no problem. I'm just slapping a little water on my face.

The two stand in embarrassed silence for a moment. Nick looks like he's gathering the nerve to ask her out.

NICK

So, it's going pretty good, huh?

NICOLE

Is it? Something feels off.

NICK

Yeah, you seem a little tense.

NICOLE

Do I?

NICK

But don't worry about it. Just take your attention off yourself and put it on Chad. Work off him a little more.

NICOLE

OK, I'll try that.

NICK

And listen, I know he's no Olivier. But he's got something, don't you think? Kind of a natural presence.

NICOLE

Oh yes, he's very natural.

Nick hesitates, again gathering his nerves to pop the question.

NICK

So Nicole . . . anything else I can help you with?

NICOLE

Actually there is. Could you maybe ask him to brush his teeth?

NICK

Oh, sure.

57. INT. THE SET. DAY.

Wanda crosses the set and assumes her position beside the camera. Wolf sits behind it, barely a foot away.

WOLF

My eye is killing me.

WANDA

Put your eyepatch on.

WOLF

I lost it.

WANDA

Is that little light set yet?

WOLF

That little light was set ten minutes ago.

WANDA

(into her walkie) Get me the A Team in here right away. Nick, Nicole, and Mr. Palomino. (to Wolf) Why didn't you tell me?

WOLF

Hey, you're not worried about the time, I'm not worried about the time.

WANDA

Oh, I am very worried about the time!

WOLF

I know you are.

WANDA

What is that supposed to mean?

WOLF

What do you think it means?!

WANDA

I don't know what it means!

WOLF

Oh yes you do, you know exactly what it means.

WANDA

I have no idea what you're talking about! Why are you—

WOLF

You don't understand me, Wanda! You have no idea—

WANDA

I don't understand you?!! All I do is take care of you!!!

Nick suddenly runs up just as Wolf and Wanda are on the verge of blows.

NICK

Hey, hey, hey! What the hell's going on here?! Jesus, Wanda. This is a very intimate scene and a lot of tension on the set doesn't help. OK? Now, Wolf, let's just go through the first part of the move. Damian, on your new mark. Good. Close-up, Damian; Ellen in the background.

Nick suddenly sees Palomino is wearing a black eyepatch.

NICK

Chad, what are you doing?

WOLF

Hey, that's my fucking eyepatch.

PALOMINO

Wolf, could I borrow it? Cause I'm telling you, Nick; it really feels right. I feel like this guy now, man.

NICK

I don't know, Chad. I don't think it works.

PALOMINO

You're wrong, man. I'm going to fight you on this one.

WOLF

Hey, it's my fucking eyepatch and I don't want anyone wearing it. It's insanitary.

Chad Palomino (James Legros) finds his character with Wolf's eyepatch. Nicole (Catherine Keener) and Les, the Boomman (Matt Grace) watch Nick's reaction.
(Photo by Bill Bettencourt)

Palomino removes the eyepatch and tosses it back to Wolf.

PALOMINO

Fine. I'll get my own. Nick, send someone out for an eyepatch. I'll fucking pay for it myself.

Nick pulls Palomino aside and whispers to him confidentially.

NICK

Listen, Chad. I didn't want to say this in front of Wolf but it makes you look a little . . . gay.

PALOMINO

Really?

NICK

Yeah, a little bit.

PALOMINO

Jesus.

Palomino sneaks a glance back at Wolf then whispers to Nick.

PALOMINO

You're right. Thanks, buddy. Good call.

WANDA

Are you ready, Nick?

NICK

One second. You need a rehearsal, Wolf?

WOLF

Let's just fucking shoot it!!

PALOMINO

El Lobo!

Palomino winks at Nick and walks back to his new mark, making a barely audible howling sound behind his hand.

NICK

Call it, Wanda.

WANDA

Going for picture. Lock it up. And roll sound.

SOUND

Speed!

WANDA

Roll camera!

AC

Rolling!

CLAPPER

Scene six, take four!

NICK

And, action.

58. INT. THE SCENE. TAKE FOUR.

The scene begins again. Palomino milks his Close-up for all it's worth.

ELLEN

I've always admired you from afar.

DAMIAN

Admired? That sounds rather professional.

ELLEN

Well, then: loved. How does that sound?

Right on his cue, Palomino walks to the bed. As the camera moves into the 2-shot he begins stroking Nicole's hair with extreme care and concentration.

DAMIAN

It sounds like the champagne talking.

ELLEN

I've loved you from the moment we met.

DAMIAN

Why didn't you tell me?

ELLEN

We were working together. I didn't want anything to interfere—God!

Under the onslaught of escalating hair-stroking, Nicole suddenly jerks her head away hard. Palomino jumps up and begins pacing at the rear of the set.

59. INT. THE SET. DAY.

NICK

Cut!

WANDA

That's a cut. Hold the work, going again, right away.

NICOLE

I'm sorry, Nick. I don't know why I did that. I'm sorry.

Palomino suddenly stops pacing and addresses Nick with a curtness that is a little startling.

PALOMINO

Nick, could I talk to you a second?

Palomino disappears behind the set, a jerk of his head indicating his wish for Nick to follow him.

WANDA

A momentary delay. Everyone stand by. We're going again, right away.

SOUND

Excuse me, Ellen? You were a tad low on that take.

NICOLE

Oh, OK. I'll bring it up. Actually could I listen to the take before?

The Sound man gives Nicole his headphones and rewinds the tape recorder for her. The first several lines of the last take are heard through the headphones.

60. INT. OFF THE SET. DAY.

Nick follows Palomino behind the set, stopping just beside the fake set window. Palomino whirls on Nick and whispers fiercely.

Nicole (Catherine Keener) listens to a previous take while Speedo, the Soundman (Michael Griffiths) looks on.
(Photo by Bill Bettencourt)

PALOMINO

I'm out of here, man!

NICK

What's the matter?!

PALOMINO

I like you, but I made a big mistake taking this
part. Have someone call me a cab.

NICK

Wait a second, Chad. Just talk to me. What's going
on!?

PALOMINO

I can't act with this woman. I know she's a friend
of yours but I got to tell you: she cannot act worth
a shit! I'm giving her everything! The whole thing
I just did with the hair; did you see that? I came
up with that on my own because I thought it
would help her. But no, she's giving me nothing!
I'm out of here.

61. INT. THE SET. DAY.

Nicole listens to the last line of the previous take.

DAMIAN

God, and all this time I thought . . . (the muted
rustle of the kiss)

The Sound man stops the recorder at the end of the take,
sets the machine in standby mode, and picks up his cross-
word puzzle. Nicole is just about to take off the headphones when she realizes she can hear Nick and Palomino

talking quite clearly. Glancing up, she sees the Boom man
has left his boom leaning against the wall, the mike pointing out the open set window.

PALOMINO (vo)

Why did you cast her? She sucked in that Richard
Gere movie!

NICK (vo)

You're right. She is not the best actress in the
world. I see that now but you've got to help me,
Chad. I'm asking you to please help me here.
We've got to get through this somehow.

The camera begins a slow DOLLY in to Nicole's astonished
face. This will be intercut with a similar DOLLY in to the
microphone leaning against the wall, ending in an ECU of
the mike.

62. INT. OFF THE SET. DAY.

Camera is close on Nick and Palomino.

PALOMINO

I'll tell you what this is about, man. You know why
she took a cab this morning?

NICK

Something came up.

PALOMINO

No. She was in my hotel room and she didn't want
you to know it. OK? I'm sorry it had to come out
like this but I told her this morning "thanks a lot,
it was a lot of fun last night but let's get something

straight—it was just a one-time deal," and she didn't want to hear that. She wanted more, you see what I'm saying? It's rejection.

63. INT. THE SET. DAY.

The camera reveals Nicole now seated in her spot on the bed. She rises as Nick and Palomino reappear and approach her from behind the set.

NICK

Nicole, listen . . .

NICOLE

Nick, it's my fault the scene isn't working. I apologize. Chad, I apologize to you too. I'm completely unfocused here and I think you're absolutely right; what we need to do is loosen the scene up somehow.

Nick and Palomino stare at Nicole for a moment.

NICK

What would you like to do?

NICOLE

I was wondering if we could try improvising the scene. More along the lines of what Chad has been doing. Maybe that would help me find something.

Nick's smile of gratitude to Nicole looks almost drug-induced.

NICK

That's a fantastic idea. What do you think, Chad?

PALOMINO

Hey, that's the only way I can work. Let's take it apart, let's cut loose.

NICK

Good! And we'll shoot it! Hell, why not?!

PALOMINO

Roll that motherfucking camera, Wolfie!

WOLF

Kiss my ass!

Although Wolf says this quite loud, Palomino doesn't hear him because he suddenly yells:

PALOMINO

Yeah! Let's go!

NICK

Alright, now we're making a fucking movie! Call it, Wanda!

WANDA

Going for picture. Lock it up. And roll sound.

SOUND

Speed!

WANDA

Roll camera!

AC

Rolling!

CLAPPER

Scene six, take five!

NICK

And, action.

64. INT. THE SCENE. TAKE FIVE. THE "IMPROV."

Nicole stays seated, though Palomino moves around making a great show of loosening up.

ELLEN

I've always admired you from afar.

DAMIAN

Have you? That's, wow; that's incredible. But that sounds kind of professional doesn't it? Admired?

ELLEN

You're right. How does despised sound?

DAMIAN

Great! (laughs) What's it mean?

ELLEN

(laughs) It's sort of like I think you're a piece of shit.

Palomino is somewhat startled by this. He looks to Nick in confusion. Nick silently encourages him to keep going.

DAMIAN

(another laugh) That sounds like the champagne talking.

ELLEN

It's not. I really do think you are a piece of shit.

DAMIAN

No, you don't. You love me.

ELLEN

The fuck I do. I can't stand looking at you!

DAMIAN

Then I guess I have nothing else to say.

ELLEN

No, I think you have a lot more to say, Damian.

DAMIAN

Well, I am surprised you feel this way, Ellen. I always thought you admired—

ELLEN

That's not what I meant. You should tell everyone what you just told Nick behind the set.

DAMIAN

Hey, this isn't part of the scene.

ELLEN

Say it anyway: The reason this scene isn't working is because you and I slept together last night. Did everyone hear that?! I fucked Chad last night!

Nick and the rest of the crew stand in stunned amazement.

DAMIAN

See, Nick! I told you this was about rejection!

ELLEN

You fucking scumbag! You think I give a rat's ass about you?! I was there to get laid and even that was a joke!

DAMIAN

You know, you are really starting to piss me off!

ELLEN

Oh, does that mean you're not going to come wiggle on the bed anymore, or stroke my hair real soft and concerned, or kiss me like a soap opera acting piece of shit!

Palomino snaps, and lunges for Nicole. She leaps to the other side of the bed.

ELLEN

Come on! I'll kick your ass! Come on!

Nick steps between Nicole and Palomino.

NICK

OK, guys, I think we can stop there.

PALOMINO

You bet your ass we can stop! Wanda, call me a cab!

NICK

Hold on, Chad. Let's just try to calm down.

PALOMINO

Fuck you. I'm out of here, man. This movie is bullshit.

NICK

Now wait a second, Chad. There's no reason for
hostility.

PALOMINO

Shut up, you fucking loser. The only reason I took
this part was because someone said you knew
Quentin Tarantino! You're nowhere, man.

NICK

Hey, you want to go? Go! I'm sick of your shit, you
hostess twinkie motherfucker!

PALOMINO

What'd you call me?

NICK

You heard me.

PALOMINO

Say it again.

NICK

You hostess twinkie motherfucker!

Palomino suddenly punches Nick in the stomach, leaving
him bent over and gasping for breath. Nicole instantly
leaps on Palomino's back and begins pounding her fist on
the top of his head. Palomino spins wildly trying to dis-
lodge her as Wanda rushes forward.

Nick Reve (Steve Buscemi) takes it in the gut for his film,
Living in Oblivion.
(Photo by Bil Bettencourt)

WANDA

Alright, everyone just stop. Stop! Stop this right
now!

As she tries to separate Nicole and Palomino, Palomino
shoves her hard, knocking her down. Instantly Wolf leaps
off the camera and runs up to Palomino.

WOLF

Alright, you've asked for it, Chad!

Palomino suddenly punches Wolf in the teeth, dropping
him like a stone.

WANDA

(shrieks) Wolf!

Suddenly Nick staggers to his feet and rushes at Palomino. His momentum knocks all three backwards onto the
bed, Palomino's head cracking Nicole in the teeth.

NICOLE

Oh, God!

Nicole rolls free as Nick and Palomino wrestle on the bed.
Nick gets Palomino in a vicious headlock and starts
pounding his head against the mattress.

NICK

You want to pick my brain?! This is the way I direct hostess twinkie scumbags like you!

As Nick continues to pound Palomino's head the Gaffer
notices Palomino's eyes are starting to bug out from the
pressure of Nick's forearm around his neck. He and the

Wanda (Danielle von Zerneck) comforts her fallen hero Wolf (Dermot Mulroney), knocked out with one punch.
(Photo by Bill Bettencourt)

Boom man rush forward and finally manage to pry Palomino free.

                              NICK

    Get him out of here! Someone take him back to his
    hotel!

As the Gaffer and Boom man drag off the almost unconscious Palomino, the Scriptgirl takes one faltering step after him.

                           SCRIPT

    (sniffling) Chad . . .

Suddenly, everything becomes quiet except for Nick's labored breathing and the Scriptgirl's sniffles. Nick leans over and touches Nicole's shoulder.

                              NICK

    Are you alright?

                           NICOLE

    Don't touch me.

65. EXT. DAY. THE STREET OUTSIDE THE SET.

The Gaffer and AC help the still-groggy Palomino into the back of the production van. JEFF, the driver, watches them in sleepy curiosity.

With Palomino safely propped in a seat, the AC goes back to the set. The Gaffer waits a moment then slips his script out of his back pocket and slaps it into Palomino's motionless hand.

GAFFER

It's called "Tsunami." A Japanese tidal wave hits
New York. You've an ex–Navy S.E.A.L. frogman,
working undercover. You save the city. You'd be
perfect for the lead. That's my number; call me, or
I'll call you. Either way it's been great working
with you, man.

As Palomino stares at him blankly, the Gaffer slams the
door. The car pulls out.

66. INT. THE SET. DAY.

Nick and Nicole are sitting up on the bed, alone on the now
empty set.

NICK

Nicole, I'm sorry. I didn't mean it. You were great
in that Richard Gere movie.

NICOLE

Shut up. You're no different than he is. You lie,
you're deceitful . . .

NICK

I'm not lying. Christ, I tell everyone how great you
are. I've got nothing but respect and admiration
for you.

NICOLE

Oh God, now you're doing your own fucking script.

NICK

Well, why do you think I wrote it?!

                              NICOLE

I have no idea!

                               NICK

It's about you. It's about how I feel about you.

                              NICOLE

Christ, did you get a bump on your head, Nicky.
'Cause you're talking like an idiot.

                               NICK

Nicole. I've loved you since the day we met.

Nicole sits for a long moment in stunned silence.

                              NICOLE

Why didn't you tell me?

                               NICK

I didn't want anything to get in the way of us
working together.

                              NICOLE

God, and all this time I thought . . .

Nick and Nicole move into a shy, trembling, heartfelt kiss.

67. INT. HOTEL ROOM. DAWN.

Nicole snaps awake with a jolt. She glances quickly at the
clock which reads 4:35. The sound of the shower still running in the bathroom.

NICOLE

Oh, God.

Nicole leaps out of bed and races into the bathroom. As the camera follows her, she closes the bathroom door, right against the lens, turning the image to total BLACKNESS.

Three

The frame is BLACK. The recognizable clatter and clunk of the FILM CREW is heard. Wanda's voice is prominent.

WANDA

Don't go out that door!

Suddenly a DOOR opens away from camera and the AC stops, a foot away from the lens. Behind him, Wanda and the rest of the crew can be seen through the door, preparing for filming. We see now the door and the plywood walls around it are FAKE.

68. INT. THE SET. DAY.

AC

Why not?

WANDA

It's part of the set, goddamnit. Now go around.

AC

Next time. This is an emergency.

The AC rushes past and a moment later the camera DOLLIES slowly through the fake door toward Wanda pacing near the set camera.

WANDA

(into her walkie) Has Ellen showed up yet?

WALKIE

ssss . . . kkkkkrrk.

WANDA

Get her into wardrobe right away.

WALKIE

ssskk . . . ssssrrrk?

WANDA

No! Scene six; Scene five has been postponed. I'm
not going to say it again; Mr. Palomino is not
working today. Now where is that smoke machine!

69. INT. SET BUILDING, HALLWAY. DAY.

The AC bursts through a door at the end of the hallway
and walks quickly toward the camera. Without knocking
he pushes open the bathroom door and suddenly stops
short.

AC

Oh. Sorry.

Standing on his tiptoes at the sink, straining to turn off
the running faucet is, TITO a DWARF. He is dressed in a
sky blue tuxedo with tails. A top hat and white gloves rest
on the closed toilet seat. Tito appears extremely annoyed.

TITO

What do you want?!

AC

I need to use the bathroom. Kind of an emergency.

TITO

Well, fucking knock!!

Tito grabs his hat and gloves and marches down the hall, the AC staring after him in astonishment.

TITO

(muttering) I swear to Christ, one of these days I'm going to punch somebody in the balls!

70. INT. WARDROBE ROOM. DAY.

Camera is close on Nicole, her eyes clenched shut as a thin white veil is placed on her head. Camera pulls back to reveal SACHIKO, the Costume Designer putting the finishing touches to Nicole's costume, which appears to be an elaborate white wedding gown. Nick stands nearby, smoking.

NICK

Just as we pull up to your apartment Palomino suddenly says he feels so sick he can't work today.

NICOLE

God. Was it something he ate?

SACHIKO

Stand up, please.

NICK

I don't know.

NICOLE

Can he work tomorrow?

SACHIKO

Turn around, please.

NICK

Don't know that either. But I'm not worrying about it. I had this dream last night where I was on the set. You were in it, and another woman, someone older. Anyway, everything was going wrong. The harder I tried to hold things together the more they fell apart. And you know what that dream was telling me, Nicole? You just got to roll with it. And that's what I'm doing, I'm rolling with it. So, we'll just shoot the Dream Sequence today.

Just then Tito walks in.

NICK

Hey, Tito. You look great, man.

TITO

I feel like shit.

NICK

No, you look good. Thanks for coming in on such short notice. This is Nicole; she's playing Ellen.

NICOLE

Hello. Toto, is it?

TITO

Tito.

NICOLE

Oh, I'm sorry.

Nick (Steve Buscemi) tells Nicole (Catherine Keener) about his Anxiety Dream; "I was on the set and everything was going wrong."
(Photo by Bill Bettencourt)

NICK

Listen, if there's anything I can do to make you
. . . if you need . . . uh, just let me know.

TITO

Put a stool in the bathroom.

Tito walks out, followed immediately by Sachiko, leaving
Nicole alone with Nick.

NICK

Did I just offend him?

NICOLE

What did you say?

NICK

"Short notice?"

NICOLE

Come on; that was nothing. I'm the one who called
him "Toto." Jesus, I'm out of it. I dreamt I was on
the set last night too.

NICK

Oh yeah?

NICOLE

Yeah. You were in the dream.

NICK

Was I freaking out?

NICOLE

Actually, you were.

NICK

That's great: I freak out in my dream; I freak out in your dream. No wonder I'm fucking exhausted.

NICOLE

Nick . . .

NICK

Yeah?

Nicole stares at Nick for a long moment then smiles briefly and turns away.

71. **INT. A CORNER OF THE SET. DAY.**

A dented, ancient smoke machine squats forlornly in the middle of the set. WOLF (with eyepatch), the GAFFER, AC, BOOM MAN, and the SOUND MAN stand around it, scrutinizing it intently. Wolf seems in an unusually good mood.

WOLF

Alright, guys; special effects today. Could be fun. Who knows how to work this baby?

GAFFER

It's the old T-160. I used it once in '85.

AC

Damn. '85.

WOLF

What's this?

GAFFER

That's where the gas goes.

BOOM

No, that's where the oil goes.

GAFFER

Is it?

BOOM

I think so.

GAFFER

You're right. It's coming back now.

WOLF

I'm going to let you handle this one, Bob. This is your baby. And Les, if he needs help you give him a hand. OK, guys? We're all working together today.

Wolf walks off. The Gaffer kneels to inspect the smoke machine closer.

GAFFER

Yup, all coming back now. Like riding a bike. T-160, 1985. 1985, T-160.

AC

Way to go, Bob.

72. INT. THE SET. NEAR THE CAMERA.

Wanda stands alone by the camera, looking around at the bustling crew like a battalion commander watching her troops in battle. Nick approaches her.

NICK

How are we doing, Wanda?

WANDA

Not good, Nick. Not bad, but not good. We need to finish this scene and do Scene thirty-one today.

NICK

Scene thirty-one?! I left my notes for Scene thirty-one at home! I didn't know we were—

WANDA

Nick, Nick. I'll send someone to your apartment to pick them up. Now, relax.

NICK

Oh, OK. Send somebody to my apartment to pick them up; it's the red notebook, under the bed.

WANDA

It's taken care of, Nick.

NICK

Good. Great. Good.

Nick walks off quickly, muttering to himself. A moment later Wolf strolls up to Wanda.

WOLF

We're all lit, the smoke machine is under control; we're ready to go.

WANDA

(hard) What about the dolly?

WOLF

Just need to see a run-through and we're all set. I'm going to make your job easy today, Wanda. Wandaful. (he slips his arm around her) Mmm, I'm glad you wore that perfume. And don't worry about Palomino; I'll take you to a jazz club tonight.

WANDA

Oh, I can't make it. I have to go see Chad; he's extremely ill.

WOLF

Oh, by the way my eye's much better.

WANDA

Listen, Wolf, this may not be the best time to say this but our relationship is going nowhere.

WOLF

What do you mean?

WANDA

Please, don't take it personally. Because I care for you, Wolf, I really do. But I've had this feeling for quite a while and I think it's time we ended it. OK?

WOLF

(pause) OK.

WANDA

I think it's better.

WOLF

So do I.

WANDA

Well, good. Still friends?

WOLF

Sure.

WANDA

Great, cause we still have to work together and there's no reason it has to be unpleasant. Give me a hug.

Wanda and Wolf move into an extremely wooden embrace.

WANDA

You're a real special guy, Wolf.

WOLF

Thanks.

Wanda slips Wolf a tender smile then walks away.

WANDA

(into her walkie) OK, let's get the A Team in please! Nick, Ellen, Mr. Tito!

73. INT. THE SET. DAY.

Nick is working with the crew and the actors. The set con-
sists of two flats (one with the fake door) joined to make a
corner. The flats are painted fire-engine red.

NICK

OK, here's the shot. We start wide with Ellen
standing absolutely still right in the middle of the
frame. You got that, Wolf?

WOLF

Yeah.

NICK

(notices eyepatch) What happened to your eye?

WOLF

Nothing. It's a little sensitive today.

NICK

Can you see?

WOLF

(snaps) Of course I can see!

For a moment Nick looks like he might snap back at Wolf
but he draws a deep breath and continues.

NICK

OK, Ellen is standing there. The smoke is flowing
in and: Ellen's line.

ELLEN

I am so hungry.

NICK

Good, Tito, that's your cue.

The fake door opens and Tito enters wearing his top hat and carrying a golden apple in his gloved hands.

NICK

You walk around her once, hold the apple out, that's right; just beyond her reach. You're staring at her hard. Harder, good. Then stop right here. Can we get a mark, please?

The AC moves up to Nick and places a piece of yellow tape on the floor. CU the yellow tape.

NICK

Then we dolly in to Tito's Close-up. Alright, Wolf?

WANDA

It should be hand-held.

NICK

No, I think it's better on the dolly.

WOLF

Whatever.

NICOLE

Nick, do I see him?

NICK

No, just the apple. And Tito, right after we dolly in give me a little laugh there.

TITO

A little laugh?

NICK

Big, little; anything you feel like doing. OK? Good.
Let's shoot one. Call it, Wanda.

WANDA

OK, here we go. Camera back to One. Action on
the smoke.

The Gaffer turns on the smoke machine which emits a pa-
thetic wisp of smoke that immediately dissipates.

WANDA

And roll sound.

NICK

Hold it, Wanda. Can we get a little more smoke?
Is that possible?

GAFFER

Oh, sure.

The Gaffer adjusts a knob and another thin puff of smoke
wheezes out.

NICK

Good. Call it, Wanda.

WANDA

Going for picture. Lock it up. And roll sound.

SOUND

Speed!

WANDA

Roll camera!

AC

Rolling!

CLAPPER

Scene six, take one!

NICK

And, action.

74. INT. THE DREAM. TAKE ONE. DAY.

Nicole stands motionless in the middle of the empty set. Her white wedding gown stands out sharply against the deep red walls. A sad shred of smoke drifts by her head.

ELLEN

I am so hungry.

Tito opens the door and walks in, staring hard at Nicole. His sky-blue tuxedo gleams in the rich light. He walks around her in a circle holding the golden apple just beyond her reach. He stops on his mark and the camera dollies into a CU of him. He doesn't laugh. Nick watches this for a moment in intense concentration.

75. INT. THE SET. DAY.

NICK

And . . . cut.

Tito (Peter Dinklage) makes his entrance.
(Photo by Bill Bettencourt)

WANDA

That's a cut. Nick; comments?

NICK

Yeah, just a couple. I thought that was uh . . . good. Tito, that was very good, man, really. You didn't feel like laughing?

TITO

I laughed.

NICK

Oh, OK; I guess I missed it. You could make it bigger if you want. And Ellen, maybe just a little more tension when you see him.

NICOLE

I thought I didn't see him.

NICK

Right, maybe you see him a little bit.

NICOLE

Alright, I'm confused. Do I see him or not?

NICK

You see him.

NICOLE

OK, what is the tension? Who is Toto?

TITO

(hard) It's Tito.

NICOLE

(alarmed) What did I say?

TITO

Toto.

NICOLE

Oh, God. I'm sorry, Tito. I don't know why I'm doing that. I'm really sorry.

NICK

Ellen, come on now; concentrate. Remember; you're marrying Damian tomorrow. You're a little anxious. You have this dream. Let's call it an Anxiety Dream, and Tito represents the anxiety.

CU Tito looking none too happy about this representation.

NICK

OK? It seems pretty simple.

NICOLE

Let's just try it.

NICK

Good. And Bob, let's really have some smoke on this one.

GAFFER

OK, more smoke.

WOLF

I still think it should be hand-held.

NICK

Yeah, well, I don't want it hand-held. I want it on the dolly. Where's my notebook, Wanda?

WANDA

On it's way, Nick.

NICK

Good. Call it, Wanda.

WANDA

Lock it up. Going for picture. And roll sound.

SOUND

Speed!

WANDA

Roll camera!

AC

Rolling!

CLAPPER

Scene six, take two!

NICK

And, action.

76. INT. THE DREAM. TAKE TWO.

Nicole stands motionless as a few more emaciated puffs of smoke hang in the air.

> ELLEN

I am so hungry.

Tito enters, walks around her holding the apple just beyond her reach then moves to his mark. The camera dollies into a CU. He does not laugh.

77. INT. THE SET. DAY.

> NICK

Cut.

> WANDA

That's a cut. Going again, Nick?

> NICK

Yes.

> WANDA

Going again, please stand by.

> NICK

OK, Ellen, good. You're on to something there.

> NICOLE

No, something's not right. It all feels fake to me.

Nick's tone with Nicole suddenly takes on an almost imperceptible edge, tinged with annoyance.

> NICK

Well, it's not fake; it's real. Just remember, you really want the apple. Tito, I still think we could see more of a laugh at the end.

                              TITO

What kind of laugh?

                              NICK

Just a laugh.

                              TITO

Show me.

                              NICK

Oh, OK. A laugh. I'm thinking maybe like this. Ha
ha ha ha ha ha ha.

Everyone watches Nick demonstrate the laugh. He seems
unaware he resembles a drunken, slightly annoyed idiot.

                              NICK

Something like that. OK? And remember, Tito, this
is a dream. Not everything has to make sense. A
laugh right there heightens our sense of . . . of . . .

                              TITO

Anxiety.

                              NICK

Exactly. Wolf, how was that for you?

                              WOLF

I still think it should be hand-held.

                              NICK

(snaps) Well, God damn it! It's not going to be! It's
on the dolly so just forget about it!

There is a strained moment of silence on the set as everyone witnesses this rebuke.

NICK

And Bob, what the fuck is that smoke? Might as
well get a couple hamsters in here blowing smoke
rings for Christ's sake.

GAFFER

The septic valve wasn't open. I got it now. We're
going to see some smoke now.

NICK

Alright, let's try another take.

WANDA

And, lock it up.

WOLF

Nick, could I talk to you for a minute?

NICK

What?!

WOLF

In private.

NICK

(sighs in exasperation) Alright.

Nick follows Wolf off the set.

WANDA

Release the lock-up. Everyone stand by.

> GAFFER

We'll see some smoke now.

> AC

Way to go, Bob.

78. INT. A CORNER. DAY.

As soon as Wolf and Nick reach the darkened corner, Wolf whirls to face Nick.

> WOLF

I really don't like being spoken to like that, Nick!

> NICK

Yeah, well I don't like your attitude!

> WOLF

I don't have an attitude!

> NICK

The hell you don't! Every time I ask you to do something all I get is No, No, No and I'm sick of it! I hired you to do a job; if you're not going to do it you better let me know right now!

Wolf is about to yell back at Nick when suddenly he stops and lets out a deep, painful sigh.

> WOLF

I'm sorry, Nick. I'm going through some heavy shit.

> NICK

What do you mean?

WOLF

I can't really go into it. It's pretty heavy.

NICK

Personal?

Wolf makes a slight motion with his head toward Wanda who is standing some distance away watching them. Seeing the two men looking at her Wanda shoots them a hard glare which prompts Wolf and Nick to turn away quickly.

WOLF

Personal, professional, emotional. It's doing a number on me. And now you're telling me you're going to fire me.

NICK

I didn't say that, Wolf. Come on, I'm not going to fire you. You're doing a great job here.

WOLF

Am I?

NICK

Yeah, I don't know what I'd do without you, man. You've got a great eye. I just hope it's not the one under that eyepatch.

Nick lets out a tense, strained laugh but Wolf's only response is to stare back at him sadly.

NICK

Listen, Wolf. Let me tell you one thing I've

learned; sometimes you just have to roll with things. You know?

WOLF

You're right.

NICK

Roll with it, man. You'll be OK.

Wolf lets out another deep sigh.

WOLF

Thanks, bro.

79. INT. A CORNER OF THE SET. DAY.

The Gaffer, Boom man, and AC kneel around the smoke machine. A can of gas and a quart of oil stand beside them.

BOOM

That's where the oil goes.

GAFFER

No, that's where the gas goes.

BOOM

I'm tellin' you, Bob. That's where the oil goes.

SOUND

Lester, don't you think Bob knows where the oil goes?!

GAFFER

I don't remember using oil in '85.

AC

Maybe both the oil and gas go in there?

The Gaffer and Boom man turn and look at the AC for a long moment.

BOOM

I think he's right.

GAFFER

I think he is too. OK, three parts gas, one part oil.

The Gaffer and Boom man pour liberal amounts of gas and oil into the T-160.

80. **INT. THE SET. DAY.**

Nick rushes up to his position by the camera.

NICK

Is my notebook here yet, Wanda?

WANDA

Any minute, Nick.

NICK

Good. Call it, Wanda.

WANDA

Going for picture. Lock it up. And roll sound.

SOUND

Speed!

WANDA

Roll camera!

AC

Rolling!

CLAPPER

Scene six, take three!

NICK

And, action.

81. INT. THE DREAM. TAKE THREE.

Nicole stands motionless in her white wedding dress, looking genuinely alarmed, possibly because of the huge clouds of smoke now spewing out of the panting smoke machine.

ELLEN

I am so hungry.

Tito enters, stares at her hard and walks around her in a circle holding the apple just beyond her reach. The smoke is so thick both of them are barely visible. Just as Tito gets to his mark the smoke machine backfires with a tremendous explosion and begins filling the room with dense, blinding smoke.

82. INT. THE SET. DAY.

The smoke blanks out the entire frame. Frantic shouts are heard from unseen bodies.

NICK

Cut! Cut! Cut!

WANDA

Turn it off! Turn it off!

GAFFER

I can't find the switch!

WOLF

Pull the plug! Bob! Pull the plug!

WANDA

Open the door! Get some water!

GAFFER

I got it! I got it!

The smoke machine emits a loud hiss and dies, filling the room with sudden silence. Slowly the smoke begins to clear as the crew moves around muttering and coughing.

WANDA

Clear the set! Ellen! Tito! Please step off the set!

TITO (vo)

I'm off the set!

NICOLE (vo)

So am I.

WANDA

Then who is that? Who is that? Please step off the set!

A pair of fuzzy-slippered feet enter the smoky frame. The camera BOOMS up, passing over a woman's bare shins, a flowered, blue silk housecoat until finally coming to rest on the pleasantly smiling face of CORA. This is the same woman who played Ellen's Mother in Part One; she is dressed exactly the same as she was in their scene. The camera pulls back to reveal JEFF the Intern standing nervously beside her with a red notebook in his hands.

CORA

Hi, Nicky.

Nick gapes in utter astonishment.

NICK

Mom!

83. INT. THE SET PRODUCTION OFFICE. DAY.

Wanda speaks urgently into the phone while Nicole stands beside her. Jeff (still wearing his hat) waits at a distance clutching Nick's red notebook.

WANDA

Cora Reve, R-E-V-E. Blue housecoat, blue slippers. How do I know? Because she's sitting ten feet away from me. Well sweetheart, that's going to be a real fucking problem.

Nicole turns away and walks past Jeff to the Craft Service table.

JEFF

She was waiting outside Nick's apartment when I went to pick up his notebook. She said she was looking for him so I figured I should just bring her up here. You look really pretty in that dress.

Nicole nods politely then looks to the Makeup corner where Nick sits talking earnestly to his mother.

84. INT. MAKEUP CORNER.

NICK

How did you get here?

CORA

I took a bus in; went right to your apartment.

NICK

How did you get out of your room?

CORA

Oh, I just went right through the door.

NICK

It was unlocked!?

CORA

No, it was locked. I just went through it. It's something I've learned to do, Nicky. I can walk through just about anything; like air.

NICK

Mom, you've got to stop doing this. I'm serious. I'm a little upset with you. You could have gotten lost, or hurt.

CORA

I wanted to see you. I've missed you.

NICK

I know, Mom; I've missed you too. But it's not really a good time.

Nicole approaches, holding up the hem of her wedding gown. There is a subtle tension smoldering between her and Nick.

NICOLE

They're sending a car. It should be here in a couple of hours. They didn't even know she was gone.

NICK

Jesus, I don't believe this.

CORA

I'm sorry, Nick. If I knew there was going to be a wedding I would have worn my fucking hat.

85. INT. THE SET. DAY.

The camera holds on Tito pacing slowly, alone on the set. He is smoking fiercely, holding his top hat with one hand. Suddenly he begins laughing in a loud, stage bellow.

86. INT. A CORNER OF THE SET. DAY.

Nick sets a chair for his mother and helps her sit down. Nicole joins Tito on the set and talks quietly to him.

NICK

There. How's that, Mom? Can you see?

CORA

Is the little fellow going to do gymnastics?

Tito glances up at her quickly.

NICK

Shhhh! No. Now come on, Mom. You've got to be quiet. Absolutely quiet. OK?

CORA

(whispers) OK.

87. INT. THE SET. NEAR THE CAMERA. DAY.

Wanda and Wolf stand beside each other in tense, awkward silence for a long moment.

WANDA

How are you doing?

WOLF

Good; real good.

Wolf looks as if he's about to burst into tears as Nick walks up.

NICK

How's the smoke machine?

WANDA

It's dead, Nick. I've got calls out to every Effects house in the city but I just can't seem to locate—

NICK

Forget it. We'll shoot without it.

WANDA

But Nick, it's a Dream Sequence.

                                NICK

That's the way it goes, Wanda. We're just going to
have to roll with it. Nothing else we can do. We've
got to roll with it, right, Wolf?

Wolf meets Nick's eyes and gives an extremely melancholy
nod. Nick turns to address Nicole and Tito and the edge
immediately slips back into his voice.

                                NICK

OK, here we go. Ellen, you've got to keep reaching
for that apple. I don't feel that you really want it.
I mean, Christ, how many times do I have to tell
you!

Nicole glares at Nick for a moment then abruptly turns
and walks off the set. Nick stares after her in confusion
then quickly follows her.

                            WANDA

Everyone stand by. Nobody move. Going again,
right away.

88. EXT. STREET. NYC. DAY.

Nicole stands with her back to the camera as Nick strides
up to her with impatience.

                            NICK

Alright, Nicole. What's the matter?

                        NICOLE

You tell me! You're the one with the bug up your
ass!

NICK

Now wait just a second!

NICOLE

You've been picking on me all day! I can't do anything right!

NICK

I'm sorry if I was short with you, Nicole, but I
think you can see I'm under a little pressure here.
I'm shooting a Dream Sequence without a smoke
machine, my mother's out there thinking she's at
a circus wedding and you tell me the whole movie
seems fake!

NICOLE

I never said that!

NICK

You did too. You said, "Everything feels fake."

NICOLE

I meant me! I feel fake! Everything I'm doing feels
fake. I can't act. I should just do shower scenes in
Richard Gere movies for the rest of my life!

NICK

Nicole, that's ridiculous. You're a fantastic actress. All you have to do is show me you want that
apple more than anything else in the world; don't
give up. Understand? You cannot give up.

NICOLE

OK.

Suddenly Wanda yells out.

> **WANDA**
>
> Ready, Nick?!

> **NICK**
>
> Ready!

89. INT. THE SET. DAY.

Nick rushes back onto the set.

> **NICK**
>
> OK, here we go. Everybody focus, concentrate. And Tito, we're still looking for that little laugh, pal. OK? Call it, Wanda!

> **WANDA**
>
> Picture's up. There will be no smoke in this scene. No smoke. No smoke in the Dream Sequence. And roll sound.

> **SOUND**
>
> Speed!

> **WANDA**
>
> Roll camera!

> **AC**
>
> Rolling!

> **CLAPPER**
>
> Scene six, take four!

NICK

And, action.

90. INT. THE DREAM. TAKE FOUR. DAY.

Nicole stands motionless in her wedding gown.

ELLEN

I am so hungry.

Tito walks in, stares at her hard, then walks around her once with the golden apple just beyond her outstretched hands. He stops and the camera dollies into his CLOSE-UP. Nick watches in hopeful expectation. He waits and waits but Tito does not laugh.

Just then the door in the rear set wall opens and Cora steps in, looking oddly puzzled.

CORA

Oh, I thought this was the TV room.

91. INT. THE SET. DAY.

NICK

Cut!

WANDA

That's a cut. Going again, right away.

92. INT. OFF THE SET. DAY.

Nick escorts his mother back to her chair.

NICK

Mom, listen to me. I don't want you to move from this chair. Do you understand?

>   CORA
>
> Oh Jesus, you sound just like your father . . .

>   NICK
>
> Mom, I'm serious.

>   CORA
>
> OK, OK. I won't move.

>   NICK
>
> Thank you.

93. INT. THE SET. DAY.

Nick walks back on the set and addresses Nicole and Tito.

>   NICK
>
> OK, good. Very good. (laughs) Tito, I think we're
> having a little communication problem here. All I
> want you to do is laugh. OK?

>   TITO
>
> Why?

>   NICK
>
> I told you why.

>   TITO
>
> Tell me again.

93. INT. OFF THE SET. DAY.

Wolf (still wearing his eyepatch) walks over and sits quietly in a chair beside Cora. He does not speak to her and

gazes blankly out at Nick, Tito, and Nicole on the set some distance away. Cora however stares at the side of his head with such intensity Wolf can't help but turn to her.

Cora still doesn't take her eyes off him and in fact stares even more intently into his eye.

Wolf glances away for a moment then looks back. Cora continues to stare at him. Suddenly, his eye is full of tears. Cora watches in rapt silence. Wolf is crying openly now. Cora reveals no hint of emotion as she reaches out and gently lifts the eyepatch off of his eye. A tight smile of satisfaction creases her lips as a tiny pool of tears is released, streaming quickly down Wolf's cheek. No one sees this.

94. **INT. THE SET. DAY.**

Nick paces tensely in front of Nicole and Tito.

> NICK
>
> Look, Tito. It's not that big a deal. It's a dream, alright. Strange things happen in a dream. All you have to do is laugh. Why is that such a problem?

> TITO
>
> Why does it have to be a dwarf?

> NICK
>
> What?

> TITO
>
> Why does my character have to be a dwarf?

> NICK
>
> He doesn't have to be a dwarf.

TITO

Then why is he?! Is that the only way you can make this a dream; put a dwarf in it?

NICK

No, Tito; that's not—

TITO

Have you ever had a dream with a dwarf in it?! Do you know anyone who's had a dream with a dwarf in it? NO! I don't even have dreams with dwarves in them! The only place I've seen dwarves in dreams is in stupid movies like this! Make it weird; put a dwarf in it. Everyone will go "whoa whoa whoa, must be a dream, there's a fucking dwarf in it!" Well, I'm sick of it. You can take this Dream Sequence and shove it up your ass!

Tito hurls his top hat and gloves to the floor and walks out. Everyone stares at Nick who is frozen in stunned silence. Finally Wanda approaches him hesitantly.

WANDA

Nick? (no response) I can get right on the phone. We'll try to get another . . . small person here as soon as possible.

NICK

No. He's absolutely right.

Nick sighs heavily and sinks to sit on the dolly in silence. Wolf appears behind him, still wiping his eyes.

WOLF

You want to just shoot Ellen, Nick? She could be in the dream by herself.

NICK

No. We're not going to shoot anything. I'm sorry.
Thanks for all your help, but it's over. I can't take
it anymore. I tried to roll with it but it's time to
face the music; I can't do this. I am not a director.
The shoot is over. I give up.

Nick's speech has the simple eloquence of truth; he is not
bitter or self-pitying. He seems unaware of how disturbing
this is to the crew. They all stand around him in shock,
afraid to move or speak. Finally Wolf turns to the AC and
puts his hand on his shoulder, like a father to his young
son.

WOLF

Take the camera off the dolly. Start putting it
away.

Everyone watches the AC unfasten the camera in silence.
Nicole stands alone on the set in her wedding dress, still
holding the golden apple. Her face is frozen in dismay.
Suddenly CORA comes through the set door and marches
up to Nicole.

CORA

Give me that apple!

At the sound of his mother's voice, Nick looks up. He sees
her snatch the apple from Nicole's hand and march back
out the door, closing it behind her.

CORA

(behind the door) I'm ready, Nick!

95. INT. BY THE CAMERA. DAY.

Nick gets up slowly and whispers intensely to Wanda,
Wolf, and the rest of the crew.

NICK

Roll camera. Roll sound. Let's go. Right away.

Wolf grabs the camera and puts it on his shoulder (hand-held) as the rest of the crew moves quickly and silently into position. On a terse signal from Nick the camera starts rolling.

96. INT. THE SET. THE DREAM. DAY.

Nicole takes the silent "action" cue from Nick.

NICOLE

I am so hungry.

Right on cue Cora walks through the door, holding the golden apple out in front of her. She circles Nicole with determination, seemingly oblivious to Nick and the rest of the crew hovering behind Wolf as he begins following her with the hand-held camera. Wolf is now in his element; gliding like Nureyev with the camera. When he pans suddenly with Cora the whole crew ducks wildly and dives out of camera range.

Cora finally stops circling Nicole and stops abruptly. Suddenly she raises the apple right out in front of Nicole. Wolf glides forward with the camera, framing an amazing CU of the apple with Nicole seen behind it. Nicole reaches out, grabs the apple and takes a huge, resounding bite out of it.

CU Nick's face, eyes wide in anxious delight.

Cora takes one step forward. CU her fuzzy slippers stopping right on the yellow tape mark. Cora waits momentarily until Wolf has reframed both her and Nicole, then lets out a huge laugh.

97. INT. THE SET. DAY.

                          NICK

And cut!!

General mayhem erupts on the set.

                          NICK

Wolf, talk to me, man! Did you get it?

                          WOLF

Got it, Nick! Everything!

                          NICK

The Close-up?

                          WOLF

Perfect. See? That's what I meant about going
hand-held!

                          NICK

You're a genius, man! What about the focus?!

                           AC

Nailed it.

                          WOLF

Fuckin' A!

Wolf slaps the AC's palm, then the Gaffer's standing right
beside him. He turns gleefully to the next person but
seeing it is Wanda he rigidly turns away.

                         WANDA

Going again, Nick?

NICK

How was the sound?

SOUND

I could use another but definitely acceptable.

Nick runs up to his mother and throws his arms around her. Nicole stands beside him.

NICK

Mom, you kook! That was incredible! Did you know we were filming?

CORA

(testily) Of course I knew you were filming.

NICK

You were great, you're a natural. And Nicole, that was beautiful. Don't you dare tell me that felt fake.

Suddenly, on an impulse surprising both of them, Nick and Nicole embrace. Just then Wanda steps up.

WANDA

Going again, Nick?

NICK

Oh, hold on. Let me think a second.

The set grows suddenly quiet as Nick begins pacing rapidly, muttering to himself.

NICK

Can I use it for the Dream Sequence, that's the question. Does it work for the Dream Sequence?

Nick suddenly looks up and sees everybody staring at him; Nicole in her wedding gown, Wolf with his eyepatch, his mother still eating the apple, Wanda, the crew.

NICK

We're going with it, Wanda!

WANDA

Alright everyone, listen up. That is a wrap on Scene Six.

The set erupts in applause.

SOUND

Hold it! Hold it! Hold it!

WANDA

What?!

SOUND

I need to record room tone. I'll need thirty seconds of silence.

WANDA

Oh, alright! Quiet. Quiet! Shut up!! Thirty seconds of room tone. The sooner you're quiet the sooner we're done.

CORA

(whispers to Nick) What's room tone?

NICK

It's for the sound, Mom. We just have to be quiet.

At that moment a door opens at the rear of the set and a DOCTOR and NURSE enter. The Nurse carries an extra overcoat. Jeff, the Driver, turns and sternly whispers for them to be quiet.

WANDA

And roll sound. Nobody move.

SOUND

Speed.

98. INT. THE SET. DAY.

The camera is wide, showing the entire set, actors, and crew. Everyone stands in perfect silence, as motionless as statues. As the silence continues the mood on the set gradually changes. One by one people drift into their own private worlds of reflection.

MS the Sound man, alternately watching his recorder and his stopwatch. Behind him the Boom man holds the mike in position to record general ambiance while staring off into the distance.

CU the tape recorder spinning in quiet precision.

CU the stopwatch, its giant second hand showing five seconds have passed.

MS Nick standing next to his mother who drapes one arm casually over Nick's shoulder. Nick glances up and sees Nicole beside him, absorbed in her own thoughts. Suddenly she looks up and her eyes meet Nick's. She slips him the barest hint of a smile.

The camera DOLLIES slowly through the standing, silent group, passing over faces in different degrees of thought.

CU the Sound man's stopwatch, the giant second hand showing ten seconds have passed.

MS Nick. He is so immersed in thought he looks at no one. The camera slowly DOLLIES into a CU of him.

99. INT. AN AWARDS CEREMONY.

CHAD PALOMINO stands at a gleaming podium, looking radiant in an immaculate tuxedo. He holds an envelope in his hands.

> CHAD
>
> We have a new category this year: Best Film Ever Made by a Human Being. And the winner is none other than my Best Bud, Nick Reve!

Amid thunderous applause Nick bounds on the stage and accepts an Oscar from Chad. He stands grinning like an idiot as the applause continues.

100. INT. THE SET. DAY.

MS Nick, still wrapped in thought, his lips starting to form the same idiotic smile. MS Nicole. The camera DOLLIES slowly into her face, now tinged with a slight uneasiness.

101. INT. A CHEAP RESTAURANT.

Wide shot at the counter. Nicole stands facing a large bald man with his back to the camera. She is wearing a cheap pink waitress uniform and has her hair under a hairnet.

> MAN
>
> Had any experience?

NICOLE

I was an actress for a while.

She pulls her headshot out of her shoulder bag and hands it to the man with a hopeful smile. He flips over the headshot and looks at her credits with confused annoyance.

MAN

Yeah, but can you cook a hamburger?

NICOLE

(doubtfully) Probably.

102. INT. THE SET. DAY.

MS Nicole. She jerks her head slightly in response to this moment of thought.

CU the stopwatch, showing fifteen seconds have passed.

MS Wolf. The camera begins a slow DOLLY into his CU.

103. INT. WANDA'S APT. DAY.

Wolf stands like Thor in the middle of the Red Set, his arms crossed over his chest, his jaw set in determination. Smoke billows around him. At his feet, dressed in Nicole's wedding gown, Wanda sobs hysterically.

WANDA

Wolf, I'm sorry! Please forgive me! I love you, Wolf! Please! Give me one more chance. Let me prove it! I love you! I love you, Wolf!

Wolf remains unmoved for a long moment. Finally he reaches out with a forgiving smile and pats Wanda's head.

104. INT. THE SET. DAY.

MS Wolf. He glances furtively at Wanda with a trace of hope still in his eyes.

MS Wanda, looking off. The camera DOLLIES into her CU.

105. INT. A CHEAP HOTEL ROOM.

This is the same hotel room from Part Two, in which we saw Nicole and Chad Palomino. At the moment Wanda and Chad lie panting in the sweat-soaked sheets.

> **WANDA**
>
> What I love about you, Chad, is you're not afraid of my power.

> **CHAD**
>
> Oh God, Wanda! I love your power. It's like an afferdesiac to me!

106. INT. THE SET. DAY.

MS Wanda. She shifts slightly and glances quickly around her. Her smile is tinged with the hint of sexual pleasure.

MS the Gaffer, frowning, absorbed in thought. The camera DOLLIES into a CU of him.

107. INT. A CHEAP RESTAURANT. DAY.

Suddenly, a CU of an incredibly beautiful hamburger being placed in a toasted bun on a gleaming white oval plate. A hand places a garnish of parsley on it then carries the plate to the lunch counter. Camera PANS to reveal the GAFFER sitting on the stool. He picks up the hamburger and takes a huge bite out of it. This shot holds for quite some time as he continues to chew.

108. INT. THE SET. DAY.

MS The Gaffer. A hopeful, delicious smile spreading over his face.

CU the Sound man's stopwatch, the giant second hand showing twenty seconds have passed.

MS Cora. She gazes serenely out before her.

109. INT. NURSING HOME. DAY.

In the pale afternoon light, Cora stands in the middle of her drab, barren room. She appears to be staring at the door. Suddenly she begins striding toward it. Effortlessly, easily, she walks right through it.

110. INT. AN AWARDS CEREMONY.

Nick still stands at the podium with his Oscar.

> ### NICK
>
> In closing I'd like to say to all the people who told me not to make this movie, who wouldn't meet with me or return a simple phone call. To my favorite professor at Film School whose parting advice to me was to take a job teaching at a women's college. To Delores DelSporto, the girl I loved in high school who left me for a Jr. Varsity football player: to all these people I'd like to say thank you but I can't because what I really feel like saying is go fu—!!

111. INT. THE SET. DAY.

MS Nick, his head and body jerking in a sudden spasm. He finishes the last word of his speech in a choked whisper and the Sound man frowns hard at him.

CU the Sound man's stopwatch showing twenty-five seconds have passed. The camera stays on the watch until the final five seconds have elapsed.

SOUND

And, that's a cut on room tone.

The room erupts with activity. Everyone moves and talks at once. Nick whispers something to Nicole then runs off.

WANDA

OK, strike the set. Props! Art Department! Re-dress for Scene thirty-one. Let's go! Right away people! Nick! Nick! Anyone seen Nick?!

WS the set. Suddenly the fake door closes right into the lens, turning the frame completely BLACK.

END CREDITS.